# We've Got To Do

# Something About

# Mother!

Eleven accounts of how individuals
found solutions to the problem of caring
for aging parents.



Marilyn Richardson, M.A.
with J. Ryan Richardson, Ed.D.

Cover design: Ron Lenz

Cover photo: Jan M. Griesenbrock

Second Printing

Library of Congress Catalog Card Number

89-52180

ISBN
0-9625755-0-X

To the caretakers
who shared their stories
and to their parents

## Acknowledgments:

We wish to thank the men and women who shared their stories. Each circumstance was unique and not all aspects of the caretaking were happy, but these individuals were willing to reveal both the negative and positive aspects of their experience with the hope that they might help others.

All the stories are true, but the names and locales have been changed.

Special credit is due Jeri Myers for reading and rereading the stories as they were revised. Her careful editing was invaluable. Thanks, also, to Jean Walz for editing the early version of the stories. And to Susan Aglietti and Ila Asmus.

Thanks to Sondra Galbraith and Sandra Wood for reading several of the stories in their early stages and giving me encouragement to continue. And to Jane Nelsen and Lorene Plumb who read the stories when they were almost complete.

Ron Lenz took considerable time to help me learn the Macintosh. Lizabeth McLaughlin and Duane Hanson also helped me with the computer setup and Beth helped me with layout and paste-up.

My husband Jay worked with me throughout the entire process of collecting, transcribing and rewriting of the stories. His patience during the continual interruptions of his reading when I asked him to listen and give me feedback must be noted.

# Contents

## Introduction

When a change is necessary in the caretaking arrangements for an older adult, when indeed, someone in the family says, "We've got to do something about Mother," that moment is most often accompanied by uncertainty, pain, or guilt. For one thing, there is not always a clear-cut sign that indicates to everyone concerned, that yes, it is time to make a change. Even when everyone involved agrees, there is often no clear-cut answer as to just what it is that should be done about Mother.

The eleven stories in this book, and the sketches in the introduction, focus on the emotional conflicts felt by those who must make, and live with, the decisions about caring for an elderly parent.

Although every family situation is unique, the stories reveal some common issues including the question of when to make a change, the stress of conflicting emotions, the burden of a reversal of responsibility, feelings of unresolved anger and guilt, and the difficulty of determining the nature of the problem. They also touch on the question of nursing homes, advocacy for the elderly, and the need for emotional support for the caretaker.

These personal stories lead the reader through real life situations. They alert potential caretakers to the pitfalls and stress of caretaking and in some cases offer advice and solutions. And they reveal the thread of humanity that connects all caring people.

Chapter 1

## Emotional and Practical Concerns

### When Is A Change Needed?

Deciding if the time has come to make a major change is never easy. "I don't know what to do," says one women. "Mother is eighty-seven, and she still wants to live alone and be her own boss. She claims she has so much to do and seems to want to stay busy. But she never actually does anything. I leave her lists of things she tells me she wants to get done, like write a letter or work on her rag rug, but when I come home from work, Mother is either sitting on the couch or lying in bed. And she hasn't done a thing. She won't even go to the exercise classes they hold in her own apartment complex."

This daughter can see her mother becoming more

and more inactive. She can't help but wonder if there isn't something she could be doing to delay this decline, something that would keep her mother both physically and mentally healthy.

**Conflicting Emotions**

Most adult children want what is best for their parents, but their feelings are mixed. While they care about the well-being of the parents, they also dread the time when the parent will become dependent enough to need more of their time and care. This, in turn, makes them feel selfish and ungrateful.

Not knowing what to do when parents begin to make unwise choices or behave in what seem to be irrational ways--especially as related to eating, spending money or toilet habits--is a common dilemma.

Norma, a retired school teacher, had her mother come to visit for six weeks. "I was puzzled when we went to the grocery store and Mother wanted to buy maxi-pads. I discovered she puts them in her underpants. Not to help with incontinence, but just so she won't have to bother to get up and go to the bathroom. Of course, the pads aren't enough and she wets through all her clothes.

Then it becomes my responsibility to clean her up. It sounds like all I do is complain, but I feel so upset. Is this a symptom of senility? Is my mother simply lazy? I don't know what to do."

The tendency, and probably a wise one, is to delay making a major change for as long as possible. But eventually ill health or other circumstances will force a decision.

If children make a change in the way their parents live and then regret their decision, they are in a bind. Occasionally it is possible to reverse a decision as seen in "Back Home Again." More often, going back to the way things were is not seen as an option. Caretakers who view the decision for change as a mistake, may continue to grieve long after the death of the parent. One elderly woman repeated several times her certainty that her family, with the best of intentions, shortened the life of their eighty-eight year old mother by doing what everyone thought best--moving her out of her home and into the home of the eldest son. "Mother no longer had a place to care for. She no longer cooked meals. She would just stand at the window looking north. She seemed to have lost heart." This woman, now seventy-five, obviously carries a continuing sorrow over what she recognizes as a benevolent mistake.

## Multifaceted Stress

The stress of caretaking elicits varied responses from those involved. The parent, the central figure in the drama, may feel angry, confused, depressed, manipulated. The caregiver may feel pressured, inadequate, exhausted. Other siblings, their mates, and grandchildren are also affected.

Jane reported, "When Marsha, my sister-in-law, called to say we, meaning the family, had to do something about Mother, I knew it was our turn. During the past ten years Bob's mother had become increasingly forgetful. Marsha, the youngest, and the only one living nearby, had assumed the responsibility of checking on Mother. She phoned her two or three times a day, reminding her to eat, talking to her about what clothes to wear, arranging for her to participate in Senior Citizen's activities, reminding her that the bus would come in an hour, things like that. Now Marsha herself was ill and had to spend most of each day in bed. Though we lived 1200 miles away, Bob and I said we would take Mom. It seemed the best alternative.

"Marsha, even though it was essential for her own health, hated to have her mother leave. She knew she wouldn't be able to visit. Concerned about her mother's feelings, Marsha thought it would be best if everyone maintained the polite fiction that Mother was just coming for a visit. But after three weeks of constant questioning and pleading from Mother as to when she could go 'back there,' the fiction fell apart.

"We had Mother live with us for a year, then we placed her in a local nursing home. She was never happy, either when she was with us or when she was in the nursing home. We knew when we brought her more than a thousand miles from her daughter that she might not like it. We had no idea how persistent her misery would be. There wasn't any reasoning with her. Logic was beside the point.

"We wanted very much to meet Mom's needs, but found ourselves unable to do so. Both my husband and I felt extremely emotional about this and continued to agonize over our decisions for four years, right up until the time she died."

**Reversal of Responsibility**

The catch-phrase "parenting one's parent" is not an accurate statement. One does not become a parent to one's parent, because nothing can change the status of being the parent or the child. What does change is the degree of responsibility and care needed, and who is to be responsible and provide the care. This reversal produces unsettling and trying situations.

It is a mistake to treat the elderly as if they were children and had not had a lifetime of experiences behind them. The behavior may be childlike, but the person is not a child and will not respond as a child would.

And there are, of course, different reactions. Some parents try to hide their forgetfulness, their failing health, their loneliness. Others become negative and demanding. Some adult children interfere inappropriately. Coming to visit they may see spoiled food or an accumulation of mail and decide to clean, to make order. They throw away papers. They determine that certain items--old clothing, knickknacks, magazines--are junk and discard them.

One woman told of going to visit and finding most of her mother's clothes spread out around the bedroom--on one of the twin beds, or hanging on cupboard door pulls or draped over chairs. Thinking she would be helpful, she offered to put things away. Happily, she noticed the flash of panic in her mother's eyes and changed the subject. Later she realized that only by seeing the clothing could her mother remember what she had.

Both children and parents are concerned when they realize the elderly person is experiencing a diminishing of responsibility, a limiting of activity, a narrowing of the mental and emotional responses. Sometimes this leads the caregivers to build a helplessness trap and catch the elderly person in it. Occasionally the older parent will build a helplessness trap and enmesh the rest of the family. A nineteen year old granddaughter told this story. "Grandma came to live with us. She couldn't get around and soon became bedridden. She needed help to do everything. One day I was home alone with Grandma when the dishwasher suddenly began to leak water. I grabbed a mop and tried to control the flood. Just then Grandma called out requesting help to get to the bathroom. I told her she would have to wait a minute. Grandma called again. Again, I told her to wait. Finally Grandma muttered, 'I guess I'll have to do this by myself,' and she got up and made her way into the bathroom without any assistance. She hadn't done that in a year."

Everyone in a family hates and resents such a situation. They feel they are being controlled and manipulated, and feel powerless to change things without either outside intervention or some kind of catastrophic event occurring within the family.

**Unresolved anger or guilt**

"Mother lives six hundred miles from me. My sister Verna lives close by and has the primary responsibility of checking on her. When Verna calls, I can hear stress in her voice. She sounds like she wants me to do something. But what can I do? I'm way out here. Verna is a school principal and a rather bossy person. I think she is unduly upset when Mother doesn't respond to her suggestions. And I think somehow she wants it to be my fault."

Childhood jealousies and rivalries that have not been laid to rest and replaced by adult relationships--the old fights for attention, power, status--may surface around the issue of who and how parents should be cared for. Questions such as who makes the decisions, how the decisions should be made, who is or is not consulted, how money is spent and what it is spent on are all subjects of argument and contention. Two adult sisters admitted that taking turns caring for their father nearly destroyed their relationship as sisters. Renee complained, "Lois would walk behind Dad and push him, trying to get him to hurry. That made me furious." Lois countered, "Renee would let Dad sit for hours. She never tried to stimulate him. No wonder Dad lost his will to live."

The stories "Ripples" and "Back Home Again: the Daughter's Story" reveal sibling conflicts. "Shared Caring," in contrast, gives a picture of complete cooperation.

There may be honest differences of opinion as to whether Dad is better off living in a nursing home or happier living with one of his children, as revealed in "Live With Me, Dad." However, these differences can easily turn into a battleground upon which sibling issues are once again being fought.

In addition to sibling rivalry, a child may harbor anger toward a parent. Or, as is sometimes the case, anger may develop due to the difficulty inherent in the caretaking situation. A child who has never gotten along with a parent would find it impossible to have that parent move in. But they may also feel guilt if they ignore the needs of the parent or place them in a nursing home.

It may be that the parent is the one with unresolved anger. And anger may result in depression, bitterness, aggression, etc. "Grandmother was not a pleasant person. She was critical, abrasive and demanding. Having her in our home drove the family apart. I was in high school when she came and had to give up my room for her. I didn't mind that except when she was so domineering.

"This may seem like a silly example, but we had two dogs, Topsy and Brownie. Grandmother took a liking to Topsy. Gradually it became apparent that no one in the family wanted to take care of 'Grandma's dog.' I first realized the extent of my own anger when I was out walking Topsy. I yanked extra hard on the lease and shouted at her. At that moment I realized I was taking out my frustrations on a poor, innocent animal because I couldn't yank and yell at Grandmother.

"We didn't realize how divisive her presence was until she went to live with another of her children. Then, gradually, we all came back to communicating and behaving in the way we had before she moved in."

Trying to balance family needs is never easy, as portrayed in "Mother's Last Days." "Put Her In a Home" is the only story that communicates, with hindsight, the wish that family concerns had been placed before the needs of the aging parent.

**Misunderstanding the problem**

"The other day, just as we were sitting down to a birthday dinner, Mother passed out. Her eyes sort of glazed, her head rolled back, and she stopped breathing for a few seconds. We called the paramedics and they took her to the emergency room. The doctor wrote on the report, 'temporary unconsciousness' but he didn't give a reason. I can tell Mother is afraid it might happen again. She is afraid to go out of the house now; afraid to be active. We didn't talk about it, but we are wondering if Mother needs to move in with one of us."

The doctor's report gave no clear indication as to how the family should respond. Without specific information it is easy to overreact or underreact to such a frightening experience. Those concerned wonder, is it safe for the parent to be alone? They wonder, is now the time to make a change in their mother's care?

Another example of the difficulty of understanding the problem comes in labeling behaviors. "The doctor felt Mother was senile, but the nursing staff said she had many of the symptoms of Alzheimers.

Who's right and what difference does it make?" asked one woman. Children may be told that a parent has Alzheimers, a disease which is progressive and incurable, when in fact the symptoms may be a result of depression or the side effects of medication. Because the treatments for these problems are so different, the stakes in identifying the real cause are high. The wrong treatment will have long-term effects on the parent.

Multiple causality, a concept meaning that any behavior can be caused by several different things, applies here. Trying to determine the true cause of the behavior is crucial. The chapters "Shared Caring," "Dignity in the Home," and "Mom, then Dad," all mention problems with misdiagnosis or the difficulty of balancing medications.

**The Nursing Home--Unrealistic Expectations**

Family members often have different and unrealistic views of what a nursing home can or should do. "Live With Me, Dad" is the only story included that addresses this problem, but it is common to hear complaints about the inadequacies of nursing homes. It may be, in fact, that the expectations are unreasonable and colored by intense emotions.

A nursing home staff is responsible for the physical and medical care of residents, their mental health and usually most of their social activities. Many employees work for little more than minimum wage in a setting that requires a great deal of tolerance, empathy, understanding, kindness, gentleness, and patience.

Most nursing homes do not have regular in-service training for their professional staff, and almost none have ongoing training for their non-professional staff. It is too expensive. Some facilities have dedicated professional staffs, devoted non-professional employees, and excellent volunteer programs. They make every effort to ensure that the home is a healthy and a happy place for the residents. Not all nursing homes do such a good job.

Many requests for special services for patients, such as health food, daily massage, or counseling, are desirable and have merit. Family members who know that certain routines, or special kinds of food, or regular attention to mental health problems are necessary for the well-being of their relative, feel frustrated and angry with the staff when their requests are not carried out. They should not stop trying.

Many nursing home administrators believe it is their job to care for as many residents as they can, as efficiently and as economically as possible. With so many complaints about the cost of care they try to do as much for as little cost as they can. There is not much room in an economy budget for individual meals and special arrangements for particular patients.

Sensitive and caring professionals do offer creative solutions for their clients. "Mother had been trying to die for about three days," reported one fifty-nine year old man. "My brother, my nineteen year old daughter and I traded off being at her bedside. Mom hated having to wear a diaper, and spent a great deal of energy fussing with it, pulling and tugging at it restlessly. At about 2:30 a.m. of the second day I went down to discuss with the night supervisor how to help Mom's last hours to be more comfortable. As we talked the nurse remarked, 'For every problem there is a solution.'

"She consulted with her staff and then suggested it would be acceptable for Mom to have a diaper placed flat under her and not draw it up between her legs. Another diaper could be laid over her to keep the sheet dry. This greatly reduced Mom's frustration and helped her to relax."

For the most part the general population has a negative view of nursing homes. However, one ninety-four year old nursing home resident confided, "It saddens me to hear people say they *had* to put someone in a nursing home. They didn't *have* to. They had a choice. I put myself here on a three month trial basis. I knew after three weeks that this was the right place for me. I've been here six years now and I love it."

**Advocacy for the infirm**

Advocates and intermediaries must speak for the aged when they can no longer speak for themselves. When illness or medication makes an elderly person unable to think and act clearly in his or her own best interest, someone must intercede, question procedures, challenge routines. Both of the stories "Dignity in the Home," and "Mom, Then Dad," speak directly to this problem.

Uncritical acceptance of advice from the doctor is a common phenomenon. Accepting the doctor's view that nothing can be done, or that a particular medication is the only choice, regardless of side effects, occurs more often than not. Nursing home procedures and routines are not engraved in stone, nor are doctor's opinions and edicts handed down from on high. They may be questioned, changed or modified. The staff and administration may resist suggestions and requests, but caregivers have a responsibility to patients to suggest improvements.

Chapter 2

## Back Home Again: The Mother's Story

Ethyl, age seventy-six, is a short, round-shouldered, round-faced, pleasant woman. She laughed often and easily as she told her story. Her easy going, mild-mannered personality explains, perhaps, her willingness to accept the advice of her doctor and her children. In the end, she surprises everyone, including herself.

In January of 1980 I got sick. I was sixty-eight years old at that time. The doctors couldn't figure out what was wrong. Neither could I. In looking back, it was probably the medication I took for high blood pressure and the ampicillin and prednisone they gave me for my walking pneumonia. I had a terrible reaction to these drugs that affected my pancreas, my liver, and my heart.

I was finally diagnosed as having diabetes and

went on insulin immediately. It took a while to get the insulin regulated, but once I did I was fine.

I had gotten to feeling better, and my husband and I were both enjoying doing volunteer work for our church. Then Leonard had a fatal heart attack. Fifteen years earlier he had had a serious heart attack. He prayed then to be able to live long enough to raise our youngest children, a daughter, almost ten, and a son who was fifteen. His prayer was answered. He was like the king in the Bible who didn't want to die; so the Lord gave him fifteen years.

My husband has been dead now for seven years. His death wasn't as hard on me as the family expected because I was prepared for it. It was like the Lord whispered to me and told me he needed Leo.

So, although I was lonely, I was doing all right by myself. Then, in December of 1983, something happened. Right after Christmas, we had quite a heavy snow storm. I went out and cleaned my sidewalk off. I didn't feel bad; I thought I was okay. Later that evening I walked out to take a look at the stars. It had stopped snowing, and I have always admired looking at the beauty of the scenery at night, especially after a nice snow storm. I was about fifty yards from the house when I felt my heart go thud and kind of quit. I thought to myself, "Oh, you can't stay here. You've got to get back to the house." I didn't want to fall down outside. Hurrying to get inside seemed to get my heart going again.

When I told my kids about this, they wanted me to go see a doctor. About a week later, when I finally made an appointment, the doctor took an electrocardiogram. It seemed to alarm him; it must have shown something. The doctor told me, "You can't live alone. You have got to go live with your kids. You took good care of them for many years; now they get to have a turn taking care of you." I thought, "Gee, am I that bad off?" I didn't feel that bad.

Anyway, I was moved out of my home to live with my oldest daughter, since she lived near the doctor I was seeing. Moving was quite an experience. Janelle said, "Think of what you want to take with you." I was so shocked at finding I had to go live with my kids, I couldn't even think what I wanted to take. Some things I would have liked to have taken I didn't. I did take family photographs, my husband's stereo system, an old blue table that is kind of an heirloom, at least to me. My kids looked over the remaining things and divided them up. There wasn't any problem there. No disagreements. Everyone seemed happy that way. But my things were gone.

Janelle gave me two downstairs bedrooms, one to use for a living room and one for sleeping. They took me to Woolworth's to pick out new curtains, things like that. I was comfortable, but I never felt like I was home. You can't live in someone else's home and feel like it's your home. Nobody realizes this till they try it. There is a certain relaxation that you feel in your own home that you don't have anywhere else. I missed that.

I would spend a couple of weeks with some of the other kids so that I wasn't at Janelle's all the time. She probably needed the break. But all this time I felt rootless, sort of like I was just floating around. One of my hobbies is making quilts, and I tied a quilt for myself during that time. It had the design of a hobo in the center, and that is what I felt like. I didn't really belong anywhere. My children were really good to me; that wasn't the problem. I could do anything I wanted, but I would get bored. I got my pictures all organized into photo albums, and I tried to help out a little around the house, folding clean clothes, things like that. But, still. . .

About a year later I was at a family gathering

when one of my brothers said to me, "Ethyl, why don't you go home where you belong?" The more I thought about it the more I thought, "Gosh, he's right. Why don't I go home?" I had rented my house out to a nice couple. They wanted to buy it; they were thoroughly happy there. But I was really homesick and decided I needed to be home.

I learned that you don't uproot that easily, especially when you are getting older. I've been back home for over four years now. I keep busy doing my own thing, making quilts, tending the grandchildren. There are several people that check on me daily, my daughter who lives here in town, and relatives who live on either side of me.

Sometimes I forget to eat breakfast as soon as I should, and then I have trouble with the diabetes. I get sick to my stomach and throw up. My daughter Maria calls me practically every day to remind me not to get involved with my projects before I eat breakfast. Occasionally I get sweaty, and then I know my blood sugar is low. That diabetes is sometimes hard to control.

My advice, if you are worried about someone who is older and needs care, is that you try to arrange for someone who lives close, family or neighbors, to check up on that person regularly. But leave that elderly person in his or her own home. It really helps to keep independent and take care of yourself. Otherwise you might just sit in a corner and feel sorry for yourself. I keep busy piecing quilts. I give them away. People ask, "Can you afford to do that?" "Well, sure," I say, "it's cheaper than any other kind of medicine."

# Chapter 3

## Back Home Again: The Daughter's Story

Janelle, age fifty-four and the oldest of eight, reared six children of her own. Four of them were married, and all of them were independent at the time of this story. Janelle seemed at ease with herself and life. She candidly revealed the conflicts she felt when her widowed mother moved into her home.

I was helping my daughter after the birth of her child when my mother and my sister Maria came to visit. Mother, who has diabetes and heart problems, wasn't feeling very well. Maria lives in the same town as Mother, and had been looking after her, checking on her, seeing to her needs. Maria took me aside and said, "Mother isn't well enough to care for herself. It is your turn; I've done all I can." She then reminded me of my deathbed promise to Dad, that I would take care of Mother.

When I left to return home a few days later, I took Mother with me. I hadn't been around Mother much, but I could see that what Maria was saying was true. Mother didn't look well. She wasn't thinking straight and became confused easily. She would panic if her meals weren't on time. Of course, with diabetes regular meals are extremely important.

Mother had been seeing a doctor in the office where I work, so I took her in for a checkup. After the examination, while Mother was getting dressed, the doctor called me in. In a very stern voice he told me that my mother had gone down hill these past few months. He explained that when one partner in a close relationship dies, the effect on the remaining spouse can seriously affect the other's health. He said the medical professional doesn't really understand why this is true, but concluded by stating emphatically, "Your mother shouldn't be living alone. She must move in with someone or someone must move in with her!" This came as a surprise to me because Dad had been gone for three years and Mother seemed to be doing fairly well.

I immediately called a family meeting. My brothers and sisters (husbands and wives felt they shouldn't be involved) came, and we all agreed. My husband and I live in a large house and my children were gone. It seemed logical for Mother to come stay with me. There was no question about what should happen. I was responsible for Mother and we had the room.

We were all concerned about helping Mother feel she had a place where she belonged. Everyone, especially Mother, remembered what had happened to Grandpa when the family sold his home and he began living with his sons and daughters. He felt heartbroken, uprooted, with no place to call his own. It was traumatic for him.

We didn't want this to happen to Mother. But it didn't seem we had a choice. The doctor had spelled things out very clearly. Still, rather than sell her home, we rented it. Thank goodness for that decision.

On the appointed day, brothers and sisters and some of the spouses gathered at Mother's house, and we divided up the household goods. With so many of us, it didn't take very long. We were anxious to make this as easy on Mother as possible, but it may have happened too fast. We had Mother packed and moved to my house almost before she knew what had hit.

When my husband and I built our own home, we had in mind adding a kitchen and creating an apartment in the basement. There were two bedrooms and a bath there already. We decided now was the time to finish the kitchen.

One bedroom was turned into a combination sewing and sitting room. We took Mother to pick out new curtains hoping this would help her feel the place was hers. We brought as much of her own furniture as possible: her own bed, her sewing machine, Dad's stereo system. When Dad had had his heart attack, he needed a hobby so he got this very elaborate system. After Dad died it was difficult for Mother to even turn this equipment on. It brought painful memories. The first time, in fact the only time I saw her cry after his death was a time I played the stereo.

My intention was to give Mother as much independence as possible. But there were things I never considered. Perhaps this was because of my own personality. I try to make things right for other people. If somebody is hurting, I try to ease the pain. If things aren't right, I try to fix them. So I had a plan for Mother. I imagined getting her involved with women in the church her own age. I envisioned her doing things with them. I thought she would make her own friends and develop a life for herself in these new circumstances. Little did I know.

She didn't seem to know how to make friends. I thought for a while that maybe my mother was a snob. She's not really; she simply has never needed friends outside the large family circle. So that part of my plan just didn't work.

Then, my mother became my mother again. You know, giving me directions: "Why don't you peel the potatoes this way?" "Did you salt this?" "How much salt did you use?" "I think you should fold the clean clothes before they wrinkle." I doubt Mother even realized she said things that began to eat at me. Soon this mothering spilled over to include my husband. That didn't go over well at all. Jim is a quiet man, but he definitely didn't like being told what to do. He had always admired Mother, saying he had never seen anyone able to stretch a dollar further. That was true. There never had been much money and she was a good manager. Besides, Mother was willing to do without. But being bossed by a mother-in-law was more than annoying. Gradually my husband's feelings toward Mother changed. He became more and more negative. This resentment has stayed with him. Even now, he has a difficult time being around her.

Then, besides wanting to be the mother again, she also wanted to be the child. She wanted attention, wanted to be babied. It got so that when she said something I had to stop and ask myself, "Is she speaking to me as my mother, or as my child?"

Mother would have liked me to wait on her, fix her breakfast, and give her her insulin injection before I left for work. But I expected her to take care of herself. I felt she needed to do as much for herself as possible. I was afraid she'd give up and have no motivation for living. Maybe she wouldn't even get out of bed in the morning. Mother told me one day she would be perfectly content if I would do everything for her, cook for her, comb her hair, curl it, everything. She'd be happy to lie back and let me wait on her hand and foot. I was still recovering from major surgery and didn't have the physical stamina to do that. I didn't have the personality for it either. So there was that little struggle to begin with.

We, including Mother, had talked early on about how we would handle certain potential problems. Mother agreed that Jim and I needed time alone together. Talking in advance, however, didn't solve a thing. From the minute I walked in the door after work, till the moment we all went to bed, Jim and I were never alone. We couldn't even walk into another room without Mother following us.

At first I didn't realize how lonesome Mother had been during the three years she had been alone. It didn't dawn on me that this was one of the reasons she wanted to be by us.

It got so bad I began over-reacting to things. I felt as if I couldn't even go to the bathroom without first checking with my mother to see if it was all right, or letting her know how long I'd be and outline in detail just what I would be doing. If I went to bed before she was ready, I felt guilty for leaving her alone. If I didn't go to bed when I wanted to, I felt angry. I hadn't realized how much freedom I had had as an adult, and I didn't like giving it up.

Jim and I began fighting. Looking back at it now, we can see it was a reaction to pressure. We could never be alone, could never be ourselves. We felt guilty if we didn't invite Mother to join us in every activity. When we did invite her, she never turned us down.

Another part of the plan that didn't work was having Mother visit others in the family to give us a break. One sister lives in Europe, several have homes that are too small, and Mother didn't feel comfortable with some of the daughters-in-law. When she did go, she often stayed only one night. Her health problems made trips difficult. Once, when she visited my sister in Arizona, her diabetes flared up.

Then Mother did something that surprised us all. One day, about ten or eleven months after she had moved in with us, she announced to me that she wasn't going to let any doctor tell her when she was or wasn't going to die. She said she wanted to go back to her own home. She got mad, and I think she literally made herself well. We didn't even consult the doctor this time. We decided we shouldn't try to control her life. If she died, well, she had lived a good life and she was lonesome without Daddy anyway.

After moving her back into her home, we took her to see the doctor. He couldn't believe the change in her. Before when he had seen her, her heart was enlarged, her diabetes serious. He felt she would be dead within one year. Now she seemed to be in better health than even before Daddy died.

This change in her health seemed especially surprising to me because on one hand she was ready to have me do everything for her, but on the other hand it seemed she willed herself well. It may be she began to feel needed by her children. Some of them, Maria for one, started having serious personal problems.

So Mother is back in her own home, has been for five years. She is lonely still, lonelier than she was before, but I have seen a great change in her. For one thing she finally got involved in an organization for women that gives her a contact outside the family. She feels useful; she has blossomed.

I'm somewhat surprised to realize I don't feel guilty about my promise to my Dad. I've spent so much of my life worrying about "what-ifs" and with Mother's diseases there are so many possibilities. What if we walk in some day and Mother is in a diabetic coma? Or what if she has had a stroke? Or kidney failure? I can't spend my life worrying about these possibilities. I've sort of let go. I think, if she dies, she will die happy. I think Mother feels this way, too.

Mother has no idea of the feelings of resentment that built up in me. I wouldn't want her to know; I wouldn't want to hurt her. Mother wasn't an ogre. She was and is very sweet. But, like my husband, my feelings toward Mother have changed. I no longer have the patience and understanding I felt before she came to live with us. I am not as kind or as thoughtful as I was before. I am no longer as concerned about her well-being. And I don't think these feelings will ever change.

I've felt the burden of being the oldest daughter, the one Mom and Dad relied on. As I said, I'm a good manager of myself and other people. Mother always seems to expect that I can handle anything. Her favorite thing to say to me when a problem comes along is, "You are strong. You can get through this. You can pick yourself up and be all right." She seems to have more sympathy or empathy for others in the family. I've always felt a little cheated in that area. When Mother moved in with me perhaps I was reflecting her own attitude back to her. I know this sounds harsh, but I still find myself saying she should be able to handle her own problems.

I haven't talked over these feelings with my siblings. We are all different, we see things differently. Maria assumes, as always, that if there is a problem with Mother, I will deal with it. Maria has her own problems and they come first.

If a situation arises and I have to bring Mother

back into my home again, I could do it. I don't think it would be easy; maybe it would be more difficult than it was the first time. If Maria sees a problem, she will call me and say, "Janelle, you've got to do something about Mother." This is the way it has always been. This is how it started, and I suppose this is how it will end.

Chapter 4

## Not A Relative

> Dan, a conscientious and somewhat reserved university student, cared for Esther M. Bales for five years. He moved into her basement apartment in 1982, receiving the apartment rent- free in exchange for doing her general shopping and being available in case she needed help.
>
> Mrs. Bales, an intelligent and independent woman, was 87, going on 88, at the time the care taking began. Dan shared many hours in conversation with Mrs. Bales, attending to her advice, admiring her wisdom. The relationship grew to the point where two basically reserved individuals could tease one another and share jokes.

I grew very fond of Mrs. Bales. Originally the arrangement was strictly a job, but I felt drawn to her. I admired Mrs. Bales because of her knowledge and her ability to continue to challenge herself. I spent many hours with her, and, because her safety depended on me, I felt truly needed. Eventually I came to look on it, not as a job, but as a relationship, a true friendship.

Mrs. Bales had been a widow for over thirty years. She had lived in this community since 1914 having graduated from the local university in 1917. She stayed involved in church and community. She remained active in her service club. I would take her to chapter meetings, leave, and come back for her when she phoned. If she sponsored a meal for her friends, I would go with her to the restaurant to make arrangements. I often had to take time off from my job to do this. I would go with her to the meal, eat with her friends, and help her get back home.

Mrs. Bales wanted and needed her independence, but I tried to make some rules for her safety. She had lost her sense of balance and used a walker in the house. Whenever she wanted to go outside, she needed someone to walk with her. Once, using a shopping cart for something to hold on to and to carry a cordless telephone, she had gone into her backyard alone. The lawn was very bumpy; the cart tipped over causing Mrs. Bales to fall and trapping the phone inside the cart. She lay there for three hours unable to get up.

When I came home the house was empty. After running around frantically, searching for her, wondering if someone had taken her to the hospital, I finally heard her small voice calling, "Dan, Dan." There she was, in typical fashion, making the best of the situation. She had rolled up her pant legs and her sleeves in order to enjoy the sun. "I knew you would come sometime," she said. After this accident we agreed she wouldn't go out alone again.

Her mind remained alert and active. The local library brought her five or six books each week. Each spring she'd plan her garden, making a list of plants she wanted before we went to the nursery. She was careful about what she ate. She had been a nutrition major as an undergraduate and continued to read in this field. Even before it became popular knowledge, she was aware of the value of broccoli, cauliflower, fish, and chicken in a person's diet, as well as the part cholesterol plays.

She also made sure she got enough sleep and, as a diabetic, worked with her doctor to devise an exercise program. The possibility of having her legs amputated was real to her. Three to five times a day she would lie on the floor and go through her routine. She may not have done the exercises accurately, but she did move the legs to improve circulation.

We talked about nutrition and exercise. In fact we had long conversations about many different things. Mrs. Bales had an excellent mind, and it was interesting and rewarding to talk with her. We treat-ed each other with respect and friendship. I knew she cared about me, and I cared about her.

As illnesses began to affect her, the demands of the job increased. Mrs. Bales insisted I not call the doctor or her daughters unless she agreed the situation was more than she could handle. She would say to me, "Dan, I am not really that bad. You know how I feel about going into a retirement center. If my children hear about this, they will put me in automatically." This commitment put me under added stress, but I agreed to honor her wishes. As a student at the university, who also worked at a full time job, I was quite busy. I did not realize until later the amount of time I gave to Mrs. Bales and the limitations it placed on me.

In 1987 Mrs. Bales developed a leg sore which almost resulted in her having one leg removed at the knee. We worked together for two months, soaking the leg and applying bandages, round the clock, twenty-four hours a day. When my work took me away I hired nurses out of my own pocket to come tend to the leg. This became a long ordeal. I got so run down from not getting much sleep at night I ended up in the hospital myself.

Because I came to like her so much, it was difficult for me to renegotiate with her daughters regarding my pay. I had agreed to do the job in exchange for the rent, which amounted to about $100 to $150 a month; so I stuck with this, even though I gradually took over more and more responsibility. Her gardener died so I began doing the yard work. When the carpenter who used to do minor repairs on the house died, I took over that job, too.

There was some outside help. Arrangements had been made for home health care to assist with Mrs. Bale's personal hygiene. Nurses would come to the home two to three times a week while I was at work. They would bathe her, helping her in and out of the tub. Having broken two ribs in 1986 by slipping in the bathtub, she admitted needing help in this area. If Medicare did not cover this cost, Mrs. Bales paid the balance.

She had one personal problem that was worrisome. She applied petroleum jelly with her fingers to help in passing bowel movements. The doctors were afraid she would get an infection by piercing herself with her long fingernails. But this was a private matter to her, and she continued as she had for years.

Her health posed some problems. In addition to the sores on her leg, she developed cancer in her female organs the first year I was with her. She had had a large cancer on her forehead removed, and although the area was discolored, it didn't cause her any problems. However, the surgery from the cancer on her female organs left a scar at the waist. Her undergarment would rub on the scar tissue and bother her.

Mrs. Bales was not very close to her children. A stern woman, she prided herself on her ability to stand on her own feet. She encouraged her children not to stay long when they did visit, feeling more independent and able to care for herself when she was alone. Her daughters were in their late sixties and early seventies. The daughter who lived in Iowa had a mentally retarded son, age twenty, and this made it more difficult for her to be with her mother for any length of time. The other daughter lived much further away. They would come to visit twice a year, at Christmas and around the 4th of July. Because of this my vacation time amounted to only three to five days at each of these times. One year I got a ten day break when a daughter came back for several reunions.

To keep the family informed of financial matters, I arranged with the banker to send copies of the checks and the monthly bank statement, not only to Mrs. Bales, but also to the daughters. They could see what checks were written and to whom. If there were any questions on matters they didn't understand, such as property taxes or income tax, they would contact me for more details.

She updated her will several times and sent copies to her daughters. I typed up a log, according to her wishes, documenting who would receive each of her antiques, and gave a copy to her lawyer. She wanted each daughter and grandchild to get the things each had asked for.

During the last few months of her life she received several well-deserved honors. I was pleased for her. Her church honored her for her years of generous financial contributions; she received a distinguished service award from PEO; and she was recognized by the university as one of its oldest living graduates. There were only seven remaining graduates from the class of 1917, and she was one of two who felt up to riding in the homecoming parade, an activity I think she enjoyed.

Mrs. Bales knew, following the homecoming parade, that her children intended to take control of her finances and her living situation by placing her in a retirement center. She had always told her children she would rather die in her own home. The knowledge of their intention caused her considerable stress. She did not sleep for two nights after learning of this and did much paper work, writing letters to people. Her daughters told me at the hospital they felt bad about the fact that this stress might, in fact, have brought about her death.

Among the letters written during her last hours was a very touching letter to friends of mine who lived near Minneapolis, plus a letter to my parents. Mrs. Bales was concerned about my career and suggested to my parents and my friends that they encourage me to get an engineering job and move away from this community. She was worried about my future, even as her life was ending.

These were the last two letters she wrote. She handed them to me, asking that I mail them right away. I did, and as I walked back into the house, Mrs. Bales fell forward, with great force, into my arms. I thought she might have just lost her balance; this had happened in the past. I carried her to the living room floor. Her skin was blue and I performed CPR. When she regained a pulse, I lifted her to the sofa and visited with her a little. Her arms hurt from lack of circulation; they had a strange feeling. Just as the ambulance pulled up, she had a second heart attack. The paramedics worked with her on the way to the emergency room of the hospital.

She had what is called a myocardial infarction. This occurs when one of the four areas of the heart has worn out and can no longer pump properly. Fluid was filling up her lungs and gradually suffocating her. This took about seven hours. She was awake and could talk, through hard breathing and screaming, up to ten minutes before her death.

She would cry out my name and ask for her daughters and for confirmation that we had finished certain projects. She was aware of her impending death and had done much to prepare for it.

The doctor said she would have suffered a less painful death if she had not been given CPR. I certainly did not wish to cause her pain. I thought that perhaps the force with which she fell against me had caused her heart to stop. I wish . . .

Even though she was not a relative, not my grandmother, I was very attached to her. After her death, it was almost a year before I could talk about it or even think about it without considerable emotion. Looking back, I think I took on too many responsibilities without her daughters really understanding the depth of my commitment. I guess I have come out of it all right, but I still miss her. She was my friend.

## Chapter 5

### Live with me, Dad

Mary Alice Shultz, an outgoing women with a variety of interests, had just graduated, at the age of sixty, with a masters degree in psychology. She became immediately emotional as she thought and talked of her father. She expressed her strong negative feelings about nursing homes and the wish that things could have been different.

My father was always a very loving person. He radiated love, not just toward his family, but toward everyone. It's as though he never met a stranger in his life. He didn't have an easy childhood. Both his parents died when he was young and the brothers and sisters were separated. They only saw each other at church on Sundays. Dad would bring lemon drops in his pocket to give to his little sisters. These days, at family gatherings, they still talk about those lemon drops. Although they were raised separately, the four children somehow maintained their sense of family and continue to feel a closeness to this day.

Now that Dad is ill and in pain much of the time his loving personality is not always apparent, but when he's feeling better it shines through.

My father took care of my mother for nine years before she died. He really never had a full night's sleep during all that time even though he had people who came in during the day to care for her. He gave her so much tender watch-care.

When she died he lived alone for a while, then sold the house, had an auction, and moved in with different relatives. He stayed first with my Aunt Betsy. That worked out really well until. . . well, he had a woman friend and I think Aunt Betsy was jealous. I encouraged Dad and his lady friend to get married. They had known each other all their lives. I even remember Mother teasing him about this woman. He had always had an eye for her; she had been an early sweetheart. But it didn't work out. Her health wasn't good and her children didn't like the idea. She was very much influenced by her children. I think if they'd married they both would have been healthier .

Anyway, Aunt Betsy started getting picky and sort of mean to Dad, so he moved in with his brother

Leo. That didn't work out either. Uncle Leo was a terrible housekeeper and difficult to live with. Finally Dad moved back to a small town sixteen miles from where he grew up and got his own apartment. My brother Frank lived in the same town and could keep an eye on Dad.

I have been going to graduate school and have been very busy with my life as a single parent, but that 173 miles to visit Dad got traveled often. I always made a point to be there on his birthday in March. I remember one birthday getting there late, after having been delayed by a blizzard, and learning that he'd been very sick. We went out to a coffee shop. I told him then, "Dad, I never want you to go to a nursing home. I want you to come live with me." I. . . I'm sorry, . . . this is hard for me even now. Things didn't turn out that way.

About a year or so later my daughter Carrie and I went to visit him. It was during Christmas break and we took Dad out to dinner. We had a really nice time. There is a very posh restaurant, believe it or not, in this little town in Iowa. But Dad was chilly and he didn't feel all that well. It was a cold, blustery day and--I don't know if it was the weather or if it was something else--anyway, Dad caught a cold. Then his prostate cancer started acting up and he was taken for radiation treatments. Those treatments at his age--he was in his early eighties--just took him downhill. Another sad thing was, he didn't tell me till much later that he'd had his testicles removed. He's had no counseling with this and that is not right.

Carrie and I went back for another visit in January armed with my "miracle"--my $500 miracle juicer. I wanted to feed him carrot juice and vitamins and all kinds of good things. When we got there Dad was much worse than we expected. He was so weak, and so helpless. He couldn't even roll over in bed. My poor brother Frankie was coping with this alone.

Carrie and I insisted on putting him in the hospital. If I had to do it over again I don't know what I'd do. You see, the thing is, Dad all of a sudden felt helpless. He got scared. He felt better after a few days in the hospital, but he was afraid to come home. He didn't feel strong enough. Carrie said, "We can't put him in a nursing home. He'll never get out." This proved to be true.

My brothers made the decision. They advised Dad to go into a nursing home. I pleaded with him not to do this, but he wouldn't listen to me. He's been in the home ever since, and that's very, very sad for me.

Although I am the oldest, Dad always defers to the boys. One of my brothers is a millionaire and very successful in business. The other brother is a dentist. In our family, although I have the highest

I.Q., I am still seen as "the dance teacher." No one pays attention to what I say. I have learned to accept the family dynamics. And lately, I even see some changes. My brothers are beginning to respect me. I think, now, I can be a friend to them in their lives. But it will be too late for me to have an influence on my father's care.

I hate having Dad in the nursing home because I believe he is getting really bad care. According to my standards, very bad care. I don't like nursing homes for a number of reasons. I feel they foster so much injustice. Think of the women who work there, the nurse's aides who get only four dollars, or maybe four-fifty, an hour. This low pay causes great staff turnover. Someone has said that half the workers in this situation do the work as a labor of love and the other half are there because they are desperate for a job. Those workers in the second category don't stay long.

Dad's nursing home is run by very nice people. The head nurse plays bridge with my brother and his wife. They, the staff, are fine people, but nursing homes have so many flaws. There should be better food, more help. The patients sometimes have to wait so long to go to the bathroom. They have to share rooms with people who may be near death, comatose. My father's roommate looks like he has just come from a Nazi death camp; he is skeletal.

The patients need counseling help. The facility where my father lives is a very fine place, nice furnishings, nice people. But there is only one counselor for 250 patients.

Many people consider my health food beliefs extreme. But why don't they give those older people raw carrot juice, perhaps mixed with pineapple juice to make it more palatable? Whole grains prepared so they could digest them? Why don't they provide massages, frequent massages, and herbs, and less intrusive medication?

The anti-cancer drugs they give Dad have almost killed him twice. The first time he came out of it pretty well. You see, these anti-cancer drugs cause the body to fill with fluid. Dad will gain twenty-five pounds and it's all fluid. That's very dangerous. The first time they caught it soon enough. The second time it happened on a Friday. He should have gone to the hospital that day, but he didn't get there till Monday.

As a result the fluid built up in his brain. Everyone was sure he was going to die. When I went to see him in the hospital that's the way they were talking. They said if he didn't die he would be brain dead. The hospice unit at the hospital was treating him, and the family, as if he were already dead. He didn't die, but my Dad became senile. If a medical crisis happens on a weekend at a nursing home, you're just out of luck.

I've been fighting with the doctors. I started out nice but. . . . They don't understand anything but allopathic medicine. They don't understand that if Dad had high doses of vitamin C it would help detoxify his system. They are telling me that vitamin C is dangerous. Is that insanity or is that insanity? How dangerous are these cancer drugs?

As soon as I get over this virus maybe I should have a really good talk with him. Now that my life is not filled with one crisis after another what with school and working, perhaps I should try again. I have always wanted to take Dad out of that nursing home and bring him to my home. If I could have done this when I first wanted to things would have been fine. There are a lot of alternative care choices here in Sioux City. I have close connections with the Senior Citizen's Center and know about all the programs they offer. All that was required was that Dad be able to go to the bathroom by himself which he could do back then. A bus would have taken him every day and brought him home and he would have had some stimulation.

Now if anybody needs stimulation it's my Dad. I understand that. Dad loves people. It would have been just a piece of cake for him. We could have worked things out. We could have moved to a house where he would have had his separate rooms, separate heating. He needs to have the temperature higher than I can tolerate. I understand our differences.

But a sad thing happened between Dad and me at the nursing home. I started talking to him about coming to live with me. Dad wouldn't hear of it. It got so he didn't even want to see me. I don't know whether he didn't trust me, whether it was the medication or . . . I'm sorry, but this is very hard for me to talk about. Anyway, I was told that my visits upset Dad because I always talked to him about coming to live with me. So I don't mention it anymore.

Still, I can't help but believe my father deserves a better ending to his life. When I consider all that he gave to his family, his sweet nature . . . as you can see thinking about it makes me weep.

Chapter 6

## Put Her In A Home

Mrs. Woolsey told her story several years after her mother died. She expressed anger and frustration as she recalled the stress of the caretaking experience.

If you're asking me, I say put her in a home. I cared for my mother for five years, and I think I was wrong. She took over our home, our lives, the lives of our children. It wasn't worth it.

One thing that annoyed my husband was waking up in the middle of the night to find Mother hovering over our bed, staring and waiting. We never did figure out why she did this. And Mother started using foul language. I was surprised and shocked to hear those words come out of her mouth.

But the worst thing was that Mother would go to the bathroom anywhere. Most often it happened in

the living room on the carpet or the sofa. It seemed to
me she took a perverse pleasure in doing this. Perhaps I saw it this way because of my own fatigue and anger.

My children stopped bringing their friends home. They never knew what she might do or say. And it was almost impossible to keep her clean. My teenage daughter was a big help in giving her a shower, but it was hard.

Another problem occurred toward the end of her life. Mother would take off her clothes and get out of the house. She would hide in the bushes a block or more away. Sometimes a neighbor would call us; sometimes we had to phone the police for help in finding her. This was a continual embarrassment.

We lost her once in the Denver airport. This sounds funny, but it was awful. I desperately needed a break, so my sister in Georgia said to send Mom to her for a visit. We hadn't realized that Mom couldn't handle this. The first clue we had of something being amiss came when my sister called from the airport in Atlanta to say Mother hadn't arrived. Apparently there was a delay in take off, so Mother had gotten off the plane. In tracing things back, it seems she might have gone into the restroom, and while she was there someone stole her luggage. Or maybe she just left her suitcase someplace. Anyway, when airport attendants found her, she had no identification and couldn't tell them who she was. Mother spent three days in a Denver hospital before we found her.

I know old people need help, but the needs of others must be considered, too. The whole family shouldn't have to sacrifice for someone who, although he or she can't help it, still manages to dominate and control everyone around them.

# Chapter 7

## Mother's Last Days

> Bonnie, divorced after twenty-nine years of marriage, was forced to find a career for herself outside the home. In spite of the divorce she maintained her strong feelings about the value of the family unit and her commitment to serving its needs. This included wanting to help when her mother suffered a stroke.

The timing was terrible. I suppose other people have to deal with this, too. It was right after I sold the house, just a couple of weeks. I had had to sell the house and was looking for another place to live, a smaller house or a suitable apartment. My youngest son, Jason, had just graduated from high school. Both Matt and Jason, the two children still at home, needed considerable guidance from me, and I didn't feel as if I was able to give it to them. My job was demanding. I was also having some health problems of my own. It was just at this time that Mother had her stroke and needed more and more help. You are caught sometimes, when your children need you and your parents need you, too. Someone has coined the phrase, "the sandwich generation." It seems an appropriate term. I definitely felt caught in the middle.

Mother lived four hundred miles away. I couldn't keep running back and forth, clear across the state; so I brought her to stay with me. She was here for three and a half months. She wanted to go home that last month, but by then I was in the actual process of moving from one place to another. There wasn't time to take her, and besides I had used up all my time-off from work, all my vacation days and personal leave, going out to visit her.

I wish I could have come home from work and spent time with Mother, just talking, but I was in the throes of packing. In some ways this was good for her because she could help. She could sit and wrap paper around the dishes. She could do that, pack the little dishes, the knickknacks. Still, I know she was really lonesome because, although it was fine having her in the house and my friends were good to her, she was clear across the state from her own friends and her sisters. It's. . .there wasn't any good choice. I don't know what else I could have done; she couldn't be alone.

Mother's stroke had affected her arm and her vision. I was able to get large print books from the library, and she liked those. An adult day care program was started at the local retirement center, and I had her go there to have her bath and to get her hair done. She didn't really enjoy the atmosphere there. She was not as disabled as most of the regular residents, and the program was new. Mother was one of only two senior adults in the program.

Mentally, except for the times when she was in pain and having an actual stroke or heart attack, Mother was quite alert. She kept her good sense of humor. She could see I was working really hard, not only at my job, but I was coming home to the hard physical work of moving as well. This added to her emotional stress.

It was a difficult time for all of us. I didn't want to sell my house. It held so many family memories. Mother knew how I felt; so during the yard sales and the auction, she really felt bad for me. She didn't need to but did, and this added to her own general distress. And it really "floored" her when she learned how much it was going to cost for Matt and Jason to go to college. Mother couldn't imagine how I was ever going to pay college expenses. She tended to be a worrier anyway, and so she worried all the more.

Part of my problem, now, is putting the guilt in proper perspective. I wish so much that I could have done a better job of helping Mother. She was thrown into this stressful situation, and I felt especially frustrated because I didn't have the time to spend with her. I was putting in long hours at work, all the staff was, because we were developing a new project. Then, when I was home, I was busy packing.

Mother wanted to go back to her home, but I had to put off taking her until I was settled in the new apartment. Mother's health was very precarious. I ask myself now, should I have recognized that, in fact, these months with me were her last? The timing was awful. I don't know if there ever is a good time.

I don't know if I can talk about this yet. I didn't know this would be so hard. . . . No, I'll go on.

I remember feeling so absolutely worn out that I didn't know how I was going to make it from day to day. I was feeling overwhelmed with the responsibility, and angry that I didn't have more time to spend with Mother. This was just the time Matt was leaving to go to Iowa to college. I was forced to deal with too many things at once: the move, my sons leaving for school, mother's illness, my own physical exhaustion, and feeling financially strapped from the visits across the state, as well as from paying for medication for Mother so she wouldn't worry about the expense. There was too much pressure from too many sources, too much guilt and anger.

When I did manage to take her home, she was extremely happy to get back to her own apartment.

On our arrival, however, I realized Mother was really quite ill, so immediately called the doctor. I told him I thought she needed to go into the hospital. He said to bring her to the office, not to the hospital. Thinking about that now makes me angry. Mother sat, in the doctor's office, probably in incredible pain, actually dying, and then even after seeing her, the doctor didn't admit her to the hospital.

I felt torn. I didn't want to leave Mother in this condition, but I didn't have any more time to stay, either. I found a home situation, a nice, private, nursing home, and got her settled there. Her sisters came to visit, and then I left to drive the four hundred miles home, arriving about 12:30 a.m. This was the 4th of September; I remember how hot it was in the apartment. The temperature had been over 100 degrees, and the air conditioner hadn't been on. It was too hot to sleep in the bedroom; so I slept in the living room, sort of fitfully.

I woke up about 3:00 a.m. feeling chilled. I was worried about Mom, upset that I had not thought about checking with the lady at the nursing home to see that she had extra blankets for Mother and to insure that someone would look in on her and see that she was warm enough. It was a most personal moment. I was very much in tune with Mother and thinking about her. A few hours later I learned that it was just at this time Mother died. I didn't recognize it at the time, but this was exactly the hour, the moment of her death.

The funeral wasn't hard. I was able to handle planning the details by thinking that this event was important for her family and friends. I arranged the funeral quite easily by putting their needs before mine. This came across to my daughter, Beverly, that I wasn't particularly bothered by my mother's death. She didn't understand how I could function as I did at the time. I don't know if she understands yet the pain and guilt I still feel about my mother's death.

Chapter 8

## Dignity in the Home

Ann Russell, a professional woman in the West, assumed the major role in caring for her parents. She felt very strongly that she wanted them to be able to stay in their own home for as long as possible.

My parents were a vital part of the local university. Mother was one of the first female professors on campus. She earned her doctorate at Stanford, while rearing a family. She loved her teaching and continued a long time, even into her seventies. Mother was seventy-six, I think, when she retired. She hated retiring and still carried on, teaching marathon classes in human behavior and educational psychology. She was a wonderful teacher, really a marvelous teacher.

At her funeral many people came to me and told me how she had changed their lives and how important she had been to them. I knew that Mother was extremely popular in her classes. They were jammed, always, and she loved both the teaching and the student response.

Both Mom and Dad loved theater and kept active in community productions all their lives. In fact, my folks met, fell in love, and married while they were both part of a university touring group. Dad, a marvelous comedian, remained one of the most respected actors in the community for over fifty years. Mother wasn't as good on stage as Dad was and I think she suffered from that fact. In his later years he just had to walk on stage and the whole audience would applaud. He didn't even have to say anything.

Mother, however, wrote about eight text books in her field, traveled all over the country, and was a well-known speaker. About twelve years ago she was in Washington, D.C., doing a workshop when she had heart failure. Her sponsor recognized she was ill; so he just put her on a plane and phoned us. It is a good thing he did because she almost didn't make it. In the hospital her heart stopped three times. Mother said she died three times, and I think that is probably true. She suffered a slight stroke which resulted in speech problems. She would try to say words and they wouldn't come. Mother couldn't face this; she couldn't face not being active and involved. Still, she did continue to do some teaching and got along fairly well.

Both Mom and Dad gradually disintegrated. First of all, they could no longer get their meals. I can't exactly remember when this was, maybe three or four years ago. To deal with that I first tried to find people around the neighborhood who could help, but that didn't really work. For a couple of years I would cook every Sunday and, if they didn't feel up to coming to my house, I'd take a meal down to them. At least they had one really good meal. I finally got "meals-on-wheels" to accept them. My parents weren't eligible because their income was too high, but I convinced the organization that these people needed something, some kind of support.

Mom and Dad got along all right by themselves for several years, with this help, until Mother said she just couldn't stand the meals; she was tired of them. Meanwhile, they were getting more and more infirm, less and less able to take care of themselves.

I have been the one most involved in taking care of things these past twelve years. My brother and sister both live out of town; so the responsibility has all fallen on me. As I have a crazy, wild schedule of touring and teaching, it has been very difficult. For the past five or six years I have gone to see my parents almost every day. Some days I can't. It is hard to find the time, with the kind of life I have, doing two or three different jobs. Everyone makes demands. It is hard, really, really, hard.

Dad went into the hospital two years ago and just about died. The doctor brought the family together and told us Dad was going to die and to prepare ourselves. Everything was failing: his lungs, his liver, his thyroid--a problem he had not had before--and even his heart started acting up. Dad had had a very strong heart. The doctors couldn't figure out what was going on.

Then he rallied a little bit; so I asked, "Could I take him home?" I knew Dad hated the hospital. The answer was yes, but he would need constant care. Through the community nursing services, we hired two male nurses to stay with him for twelve-hour periods. We needed men because they had to be hefty enough to lift Dad in and out of bed, in and out of the bathtub. They were equipped with beepers so that they could leave after they got him into bed. Eventually one of the nurses said he would like to stay the whole time and not have the other nurse. David was with my parents for a year.

Dad has Parkinson's disease, and the medication for this is L Dopa. One of the side effects of L Dopa is hallucinations. This requires a constant vigilance in balancing the medication, trying to give enough to ensure him mobility and yet not so much as to produce hallucinations. Dad experienced periods of hallucinations; then we would cut the medication down to compensate.

In the last couple of years Dad has not been able to walk unattended. He has to be lifted in and out of bed. He can't even get up out of a chair. But during the night, hallucinations cause him to do superhuman things. Dad was a jeweler, and one night he thought he had dropped some diamonds in the carpet. He got up out of bed and searched for them, completely rubbing off all the skin on his forehead and his knees. When I came the next morning, I saw they were absolutely raw. Dad had been crawling on the floor, in his very infirm state, trying to find those diamonds. It was extremely real to him. At times Dad might pick up the bed covers and say, "I have some diamonds here and I can't find them." Or, "Where's the watch I brought from the store?"

During this same period, Mother was failing; she began to have mood swings, a slight manic-depressive personality. This had happened earlier in her life, in her thirties, and she felt it was hereditary. The susceptibility to it is a chemical thing. The tranquilizer valium, that takes care of this, was a drug Mother couldn't take because of her heart.

Due to these mood shifts, Mother did some really crazy things. One night she climbed out of her bedroom window, claiming Dad was after her. Still in her nightgown, she hitchhiked a ride up to my house. Another time she said she was afraid Dad was after her with the gun. Dad was a hunter and he had guns upstairs, but he is the most mild-mannered, sweet, gentle guy imaginable. Nothing like this happened, except in her mind.

Mother would be either sky-high or down low. When she was high, she would do these crazy things. When she'd go low, she would simply sit and stare vacantly ahead. This was frightening, too.

It was wild going through this, trying to monitor everything. Mother didn't like any doctors. She went to one psychiatrist and then wouldn't go anymore. I found another I thought good, a friend of mine. He worked well with her for a while; then she wouldn't go back. Mother also decided she didn't want to deal with the medical doctor she had had for many years, so found another one. I was sorry about this because the new doctor was not conscientious. Later, after it was all over, I found that he hadn't followed her closely enough. In fairness, Mother had become most difficult to handle. Both my mother's and my father's personalities completely changed because of their illnesses.

Then another problem surfaced. I noticed jewelry was missing. Over the years Dad had given Mother some beautiful things. The pieces were gone, all the things that were supposed to go to her children and grandchildren. About a year before she died, Mother started giving away many of her personal things. I think she felt something was going to happen. Because of this, I didn't know whether David, the male nurse, stole things or whether Mother had given them away. This made me feel terribly sad.

Next, the bank statements started disappearing. Mother had always handled the finances; she was sharp, the business head. Dad was more passive. Both Mother and Dad were signing the checks. I was paying all the bills. When I asked David about the bank statement, he said, "Oh, I'm sure it is here somewhere. I've seen it." He threw me off for a month or so. It could happen in that house, papers getting misplaced, with all of them handling things, and with Mother and Dad getting more and more forgetful.

But I began to get more suspicious; so asked the bank for photocopies of the statements. This took two months. For some reason the bank didn't do it when I first made the request. I had to go back, and. . . it was just one of those awful mix-ups. When the statements came, it was clear that David had been stealing a considerable amount of money. Still, I was afraid of confronting him. My parents needed the care and I needed to find a replacement first. David was acting, well, not himself, but I didn't really suspect anything except the thefts.

By the time I had all my papers together, I was involved in an annual three week workshop. My sister Deanne had come from Oregon and was living in the house. She noticed nothing out of the ordinary. This guy was so sharp, so smart. When the workshop was over, we gave him notice. We had found a couple who would live in, twenty-four hours; we could see we needed that now.

By the time we got him to court, David had stolen twenty thousand dollars from my folks. I had a file this high on him: false purchases, the overload on groceries, etc. He was having Mother sign blank checks; then he would fill them in for $1500 to $2500 dollars. The bank just cashed them; they should have let me know.

I decided to prosecute. I had to work hard, but finally had a case. The city detective was wonderful. Three trial dates were set, but David never showed up at any of them. When they finally found him and got him to come in, he pleaded guilty. He was put on probation a year ago, and told he had to pay restitution for the whole $20,000. I received one $100 check. The police said it looked like drugs. I was amazed because I hadn't seen it at all, and my sister hadn't seen it, even living in the house. We learned David was on cocaine while he was with my folks. "Look at the pattern," one of the officers said. "It's a few hundred dollars more each month, and then into the thousands the last few months. To support their habit, addicts keep taking more and more."

The injustice of it upset me. I talked to his probation officer. He pointed out that the police cannot be terribly concerned about a petty criminal like this when they have many cases involving much worse crimes. Anyway, it was a whole big, time-consuming problem that was very . . . well, it was awful to deal with.

With all this going on, I hadn't realized how sick Mother was getting. She became unable to walk. We thought it was in her mind because she was doing other crazy things. Eventually we learned she had a peripheral nerve disease. Doctors guessed at this, but weren't sure. Mother went through a CAT scan and everything. I can't remember what it is called, peripheral neuropa, I think. The nerves start to die from the extremities so that the fingers and toes go first, then the elbows and knees, and so on. Mother absolutely could not walk, and, actually, she was enjoying being completely taken care of by David.

In the last month, while David was still there, Mother began to develop bedsores. Nobody told me about bedsores. I didn't have any experience with them, nor did my sister. Mom was in the hospital and then home for another month before she went back into the hospital for good and during that time bedsores appeared that were from two inches to about twelve inches in diameter! They were the most awful looking things. I talked to a woman at the university hospital who has a paraplegic husband. She said that avoiding these sores requires constant vigilance. If someone is left in the same spot for two hours, the skin, the tissue, will start to die. Patients have to be moved constantly, day and night.

David lied to us, saying the sores were getting better, when, indeed, they were getting much worse. We could never get on top of those bedsores. That was the thing, that to me, was so awful. We did everything, plastic surgery, everything, to try to close them up. They were just like open wounds. Finally, the doctor put Mother on a Clinitron bed, something I had never heard of. It is filled with soft silicon sand and is in constant motion. This kept Mother moving just slightly, kind of like rocking, very subtly. There was no more disintegration, but it just made me heartsick that Mother had been through such pain. One comfort is that her nerves were all dying; so she probably didn't feel it as much as she might have otherwise. Still, it was a terrible death. She died of them. It wasn't her heart; it was the bedsores, decubatus ulcers they call them. Oh, it was awful!

I could have taken David for homicide, but I didn't want to get that messy. It was a terrible thing, living through that, and I had all of the burden of it.

I think women are better caregivers than men. They feel the responsibility and the guilt more. Deanne felt helpless being in Oregon and unable to help. She would come up during the workshop, a time when it was impossible for me to be there every day. But my brother, who lives ninety miles away, not that far, seldom comes down. Just once in a while. He would have been happy to put them in a rest home and forget them. He doesn't say that, but I know by his behavior it wouldn't have bothered him. It bothers me terribly. I want to keep my parents in their own home as long as possible.

I am still trying to keep Dad in his home. It offers a more dignified life. He still has friends come to visit him, and he is master of his own home. It is much better now, with the new couple giving twenty-four hour care. The woman is a medical doctor from Brazil who can't practice here because she has not passed the U.S. medical exams. She is very bright, absolutely wonderful, and her husband can do the lifting. The cost is about $1200 a month, plus room and board for two.

Dad has been incontinent now for a year. He uses a catheter bag. Mother also had one at the end. The catheter is hard to take care of. The woman is very careful about it; she knows how to handle it. But even though she is a medical doctor, by law she can't change it, so a county nurse comes in three times a week to check it.

I keep telling Dad, "You are the boss and these people work for you. Whatever you want you can have." He is so sweet; he tries to make them happy. Anyway, it is working out quite well.

**Postscript** (one and a half years later): Dad died last January. He died a very dignified death, deciding himself that it was finally time to stop all treatment.

We had arrived at a time when the next decision was to put in a pacemaker. Dad asked me to call my sister and brother. They got there before he died, and we were able to say goodbye. He was gone in less than twenty-four hours once he decided to let go.

As to David, he missed the required parole meeting three times; so they finally put him in jail.

Chapter 9

## Shared Caring

> Penny and Elaine were sisters who cared for their aging mother in her own home for three and a half years by taking alternate twenty-four hour shifts. Penny was age 59, Elaine, 62, and their mother, 89, when the care taking began. Their mother paid them a salary.

P: Mother had taken care of her own mother when she could no longer stay alone. And although Grandma's body was strong, her mind had gone; she didn't know who people were. I remember Mother got "kicked in the shins" and received many a tongue lashing. Grandma just wasn't Grandma anymore. As a result Mother had told us, "When I get to that point, you take me and put me in a home. Even if you have to take me kickin' and squealin', don't put up with that. Don't ruin your lives." But, as time went on, she decided she didn't like the idea of going into an old folk's home.

E: And we didn't like the idea either. Mother had had to go into the hospital. When the doctor deter- mined she could come home again, the two of us decided right then, without talking to anyone, that we would take care of her in her home as long as she needed us. We then talked it over with our husbands and families; luckily they were supportive.

P: We didn't give them much choice.

E: No, we didn't. Penny and I agreed to take alternate days and to help one another if problems arose. Sometimes one of our kids would get hurt or sick, and we would phone to say we couldn't come. But we never had a big problem.

P: Both of us even had surgery during this time, and I had a big church job, but when necessary the other would just take over. Occasionally one of the daughters-in-law would come and spell us for a day or two. One daughter-in-law came every week and washed and set Mother's hair. It was amazing how it worked out. My church calling required considerable phoning, but it was easier to do that at Mother's place than at my own home.

E: As a surgical nurse, I was on call at the hospital from 3:30 in the afternoon to 7:00 the next morning.

P: And when Elaine was on call, essentially I was on call. If she had to go to the hospital, I had to come in from the farm to be with Mother. I only had to get up once, or maybe twice, in the middle of the night to take over. It just worked out.

P: Mother was pleasant, easy to care for. If she had gotten ornery or mean, it might not have worked. But she was most cooperative, sometimes to the point of sacrificing her own comfort.

E: Many times we would have to scold Mother because she wouldn't tell us her needs soon enough. If she wanted a drink and she thought we were asleep, she would just lie there and wait till we stirred.

P: Mother didn't like to wake us up. When we were in the other bedroom, we were on edge at each little sound. I got better sleep when I moved into her room and used the chaise lounge.

E: On the nights I stayed at Mother's, I slept on a sleeping bag on the floor in her bedroom. I have back trouble and that is how I like to sleep.

P: Of course there was an emotional drain. I felt that I neglected my own family. Taking care of Mother was a big commitment of time and on occasion our husbands got a little edgy about it. If mine complained, I'd suggest perhaps it was time to look into finding a rest home for Mother. He was always quick to say, "No, don't do that."

E: No, neither of our husbands wanted that. Occasional complaints were normal.

P: At first, I would go home on my free days and work like mad, baking bread, doing the laundry, trying to keep the house up. I would be so tired, I was glad to get back to mother's. Finally I gave up trying to do so much at my house.

E: Our husbands learned how to do their own laundry, how to start the dishwasher, put the dishes away, things they never considered doing before.

P: We could leave Mother for an hour if we wanted to walk to the grocery store or do some other errand. Still, we didn't like to be gone for long. Mother had lost her sense of balance and was always going backwards. She would have to grab on to things, and the walker didn't help at all because it would just go backwards with her. One time I went outside to do a little yard work. When I came back in, I could hear Mother giggling. She had gotten up to do something and ended up on the floor between the sofa and the television. She was just sitting there in the corner laughing and asked, "Would you help me get out of here?"

E: If we walked behind her, we could keep her going forward. The balance problem was a side effect from having had shingles.

P: Mother got encephalitis and was really sick, out of her head and everything. Elaine brought the doctor's books home, and we read up about it. We'd been warned that this would probably be the end. But she recovered, except for this complication.

E: Passing the time was hard for her. Those last years Mother couldn't read or crochet or do any of her handiwork. She couldn't even see the television very well. She had to sit very close and have the volume extremely loud.

P: That's how I got hooked on soap operas. There were one or two soaps she liked. I couldn't get away from them if I wanted to. Even if I was in the kitchen I could still hear the TV. So I got interested in the stories.

P: She continued to play Scrabble. Mother had played for years and knew many, many words we didn't know so she held her own.

E: She did everything she could to keep her mind alert. Just two weeks before she passed away, Mother had me writing down the different states as she named them to see how many she could remember.

P: She had me write the Lord's Prayer in large letters so she could recite it.

E: And the Twenty-third Psalm. I would be in the kitchen at times and would hear her in the other room talking. I wondered if she was saying her prayers, but she would be rattling off these verses. And she would name all her children, grandchildren, and great-grandchildren. She could say all thirty-seven of them.

E: In September, just four months before she died, she recited "Under The Spreading Chestnut Tree," missing just one small part. And that is a long poem.

P: Mother got up to the table for meals just as long as she could. And no matter what we fixed, although we usually asked her what she would like, she never complained. She frequently got a bit shaky, and if she saw she spilled food, she gave right in to letting us feed her. She didn't demand her independence that way. Anything to help us, she would do. It was only the last few months she had to be fed in bed.

E: As to bathing, as long as she could get into the tub, she wanted to do that. I would help her out by putting one foot in the tub to better balance myself. She would sit on the edge of the tub to be dried. Later we gave her bed baths.

E: We couldn't have kept Mother in her own home without working together, trading off days. The only other way we could have done it was to take her into our own homes.

P: I did take Mother into my home twice. One time it

was for four weeks, when she had pneumonia. But it was more difficult. She would get confused about things like what door led where.

E: And our heat was different. She was always chilly. There were drafts, and she wasn't as comfortable.

P: Elaine and I agreed that it would make each of us uncomfortable to come into the other one's home to take a turn at nursing Mother. The family members would be around; it wouldn't be as relaxed. Keeping Mother in her own home was the ideal way.

P: She could always tell us exactly where things were, which room, what corner of the drawer. We didn't dare rearrange things, or something would get lost. Mother wouldn't know where we'd put things and we might forget.

P: There were a few medical concerns, of course. Mother was a diabetic and had to have shots every day.

E: And have her blood tested each week.

P: Since Elaine was a nurse, she could do this. I, too, have given shots to family members; so that didn't bother either of us. Mother gave herself her shots until she got so she couldn't see. Even then she would have one of us put the insulin in the needle and then inject it herself.

E: Mother had some trouble breathing.

P: We used oxygen the last three years, on occasion, just when she had trouble breathing. There are portable tanks available that can be wheeled anywhere. The last few months she needed it all of the time. She would keep the hose to her face with a clip that fitted around her ears.

E: Occasionally there were problems with her medication. Mother took something for her high blood pressure and sometimes would get over medicated.

P: We had some sad, horrible experiences with that, until we found out what was wrong.

E: Yes. There had to be two of us then, just to keep her in bed. She would hallucinate and would see people.

P: Yes. People who had been dead for several years. Really horrible, scary things. One time it was someone after a baby, with a knife. These hallucinations lasted for two or three days.

E: We found out what to do rather by accident. A surgeon was asking me about mother, and as I described what was happening, he just stopped and said, "Elaine, call her doctor and have him take her off everything." We did this, but it required keeping a close watch on her. I could tell the moment she was all right again. I had taken the sewing machine into her room to be near her. It was 2:00 o'clock in the afternoon and she just settled down. The next time it happened we knew what was wrong and what to do.

P: Another problem was that Mother would hear things like bees buzzing. She would ask me to get that bee, the one up in the corner. I don't think there was a bee.

E: She was sensitive to little things. One time when Mother was in the hospital she told us something was bothering her on her catheter. When we investigated, there was a small ant down there.

P: And this was in the hospital. Elaine found it when giving her a bath.

E: During that same hospital stay, Mother wanted to get up to go to the bathroom. I was afraid she would fall. She got very angry at me, but I just sat at the end of the bed and wouldn't let her up. She was kind of "out of it" at the time. When she came to, Mother remembered how angry she had gotten. She also remembered that two people had come into the room and remarked, "Isn't it pathetic that her daughters are keeping her alive so long. Why don't they just turn the oxygen off and let her go."

P: In describing this event she made us realize it's not

wise to say something around people you think might be unconscious.

E: As to keeping Mother alive, when you are caring for someone you love and you want to make that person comfortable, you do all you can. We had the oxygen support because it got so difficult for Mother to breathe; there was a rattle in her throat. We wanted to ease this for her.

Mother could hear herself breathe and said, "You know what this is, don't you? The death rattle." We called the doctor immediately. He had been there only twenty minutes before and couldn't believe that we needed him. He put a diuretic into the IV and it got rid of the fluid immediately.

P: Mother came out of this and lived much longer; ten more months, I believe.

E: But Mother didn't want extra measures taken. Once when she was in the hospital, a nurse came in and said, "You know what I have to do?" We said no, we didn't.

P: If Mother failed the nurse said she would have to bring in the life-support machine, no matter what the age of the patient. "It is the law. I have to do what I can," she said. We protested, because Mother didn't want any life-support systems. The nurse said she had no such instructions on her orders, and she could not even call the doctor on the phone for clarification. He had to come back to the hospital in the night and write it down himself. Mother had told her doctor, clearly, what she wanted, so there was no problem that way.

E: It really bothered me, the first time I had to request "No Code" be written on the orders. That was four years before Mother actually died. I felt squeamish about it, but Mother said she would haunt me if I didn't.

E: We felt that her last years weren't too uncomfortable; that we hadn't done her any wrong by the way we had taken care of her. Mother made me promise that I wouldn't give her blood transfusions. I convinced her she had to have the IV because her tongue would thicken and she would be miserable. We agreed to do only what would make her comfortable.

P: Even if the IV extended her life a little, it seemed the thing to do so she wouldn't have all that pain to go through from getting dehydrated. We never had to give her more than one at a time. She responded to them very quickly.

E: A doctor friend said he didn't want either of us to take care of him when he was old. We were on top of things too quick. He felt it was remarkable how Mother kept bouncing back.

P: I think we hated to have Mother die because she was such a good friend, a great listener. And she would keep a confidence. Besides being our mother, she was our best friend.

E: And she kept her sense of humor.

P: I wish I could remember some of her quips. We would all be standing around her bed, so worried, and she would say something to make everybody laugh. One time, because of her need to go to the bathroom so often, she said, "I use as much toilet paper as a family of eight."

E: She let us know she was ready to go one time by remarking, "I've had my say."

P: Still Mother hadn't wanted to die in the winter.

E: It was not that she was worried about it for herself. She just didn't want it to be miserable for the family.

P: She used to say, "Well winter's here. Now I've got to wait till spring."

P: If I had it to do again, I might do things a little differently. I didn't realize how near to death she was getting. There were signs, but I didn't recognize them. Tissues were breaking down. Any little wrinkle in the sheet would make an indentation in her skin. She didn't have any trouble with bed sores till right at the end, the last few days. That was another sign I didn't recognize. She would be fine, and then the next day there would a sore on her spine or her heel. We used heel cups to help with that.

E: Even up to a few hours before she died, if Mother was sleeping, we could rouse her and she would answer our questions. Her mind was clear right to the end. This definitely made it easier to care for her.

P: As I look back, I wish I had been a little more attentive. I wish I had rubbed her feet more, paid more attention to her comfort. The night she died I felt I had neglected her. We had had a hard time getting things ready for Christmas. We had done our shopping through the catalog, but on Christmas Eve we were busy wrapping gifts. Both of us were in and out often. I think I stood there, watched her take her last breath, and without realizing it, walked right out again. Whenever Mother took a deep breath, we would think she was all right for a while. But I think the one I heard her take was her last one.

E: Even that last day, Mother's breathing was not heavy enough for us to be alarmed. I didn't notice any change. Four days before, on Saturday morning, she sat up, had breakfast, and I gave her her bath. She said, as she always did, "That sure feels good. I'll be able to rest nice, now." At 1:30 I went back in and said, "Mother, we'd better give you some lunch." She was in a coma by then. She would rally a little if we spoke to her, opening her eyes. But she didn't talk after Saturday morning. She died Tuesday evening.

E: Penny was back in Mother's room a few minutes later and called me. Mother was gone. I suppose we felt so bad because we had always imagined that I would be on one side and Penny on the other when Mother went.

P: All of a sudden she didn't give us that choice. We could have wrapped the presents after she died. But we didn't know that.

E: One of my children said, "Well, what do you expect? She came in on a holiday (Valentine's Day); she was going to go out on a holiday."

P: Would we do it again? In a minute.

E: We have no regrets.

(In settling the estate the brothers voted to send Penny and Elaine and their husbands on a vacation trip to Hawaii in recognition of their service.)

Chapter 10

# Ripples

Sherman suffered a serious stroke at the age of eighty. Speech was difficult, walking impossible. He could barely feed himself. His mind, however, was still active. For example, while sitting in his wheelchair, he talked of his ideas for a device to help the crippled walk again.

His wife Sarah, also eighty was a petite woman who had always been active and social. She felt trapped in the new circumstances of caretaking.

Their four adult children, Barb, Jill, Laurie, and David, did not agree on what was the best solution to caring for their parents. Each saw the problem from their own perspective. The family conflicts that are revealed are not uncommon.

**David:** About fifteen years ago, shortly after we moved to the upper Midwest, my parents moved here too. We lived as neighbors while building a new floral business in a suburb of a large city. They lived above the shop and we lived next door.

Our parents moving here gave us a very stable feeling. We felt like a family again. They were nurturing, caring and supportive of our plans.

I loved working with my Dad and getting to know him as a person. We developed a closeness as a family and soon our house became a central location for the rest of the family to gather during holidays.

Part of the reason my folks moved here was to help us build the business. They had always lived in a small community and felt hesitant about coming to the city. But Dad, who had been a nurseryman, came to oversee everything and help me realize my dream. He was full of ingenuity and ideas. Without him I wouldn't have been able to create such a unique facility, offer so much variety.

Mom's experience in arranging flowers and her excellent taste in gift selection was important, too. Mother, however, is not a very positive person. She is a worrier and likes to play things safe. She often casts a negative light on things. Dad is the opposite, always one to venture out, take more chances and be more daring. Together, Dad and I were able to override

Mother's anxiety and her apprehension and go ahead with our elaborate and innovative plans.

Of course there were the typical family conflicts. My parents were critical of the way we were raising our children. There was some truth to what they said. We are not as watchful as we should be; we don't discipline with consistency. They gave us good advice, but it wasn't always well taken.

During the initial stages of the planning my wife felt excluded. Mother was so involved in the business that it was threatening to Ellen. I was making all the decisions with my parents and Ellen was home with our seven children. When Mother started to phone every morning to check on when I was coming to work, it drove Ellen crazy. A real rivalry developed.

Since Dad's stroke, this conflict has been resolved. We feel, now, that living close so we could keep an eye on them has been a real benefit.

The folks still lived next door when Dad was first paralyzed and confined to the wheelchair. He couldn't go to the bathroom by himself. He had to be lifted onto the toilet. I'd put him on and then run back to work because sometimes he'd sit there for a half hour. I'd say, "Mom, just call me when he's ready." She'd call and instead of running right back sometimes I'd stay away forty-five minutes or an hour.

This is the way I am. I'm not proud of this part of my personality. I'm more self-centered than I'd like to admit, more selfish. It's hard for me to think of other people, hard to be thoughtful of my parents.

My sisters were fit to be tied at my negligence. They really got after me, demanding that I be more systematic. After Dad moved to an apartment in the center of town they said, "Just pick one day a week to come in and help." They got me organized and I went every Thursday. Still, I was often late.

Finally, Laurie really gave it to me. She said, "Don't you come tooling in at nine or ten in the morning. Get Dad up early, get him bathed, get breakfast. And don't you ever be late again." Laurie has always played an important role in my life so I thought I'd better change my ways.

I'm glad to be able to help my parents, but if I am totally honest I would have to say it's an inconvenience. Sometimes I catch myself saying, "Oh, gee, I've got to go there again." But I stop myself and say, "Now wait, don't think that. Don't begrudge them help now. If you do you'll be sorry your whole life, after all they've done for you."

**Barb**: Shortly after Dad got sick my sister Jill and her husband Art, decided to move the folks from the suburb into an apartment complex for the elderly. It's close to a clinic and to the physical therapist and only five blocks from where Art and Jill live. It is also, unfortunately, in the heart of a large city.

This move was okay for Dad, but not so great for Mom. Dad is sick and can't do much anyway. The apartment is new and comfortable and nice. The doorways are wide for the wheelchair. The tub is made for an invalid. The toilet has support bars. There are no steps so he can be wheeled to a car and driven to the doctor or the therapist.

But Mom gets really lonesome. She had made a place for herself in David's rather quiet suburban community. She had a circle of friends, kept busy with church and her ladies club. She could visit, go places. She knew her way around town. Living in the city is really hard on her. The traffic noise bothers her. She is afraid to drive, afraid of being mugged, afraid to even go to the grocery store. She has been depressed, seriously depressed.

This is a dilemma. What is good for Dad is horrible for Mom. Is that fair?

The thing is, Jill and Art made this decision without consulting any of us. They just announced their plans to bring the folks into the city. They said they wanted to help them and they wouldn't mind the extra work and the inconvenience. They would make sure they got to the doctor, would help shop for groceries, make regular visits.

But it has turned out to be very wearing. Art and Jill got burned out after a few months. Dad has to be lifted several times a day. Jill's recent health problems keep her from doing that.

Then each of them found a new job that required extra hours of training. They need the work, but this means Mom is lonelier than ever. Some of the positives have evaporated.

We have talked about possible alternatives, but there don't seem to be any. David lives in a suburb nearby, but he and Ellen have a large family and a florist shop that keeps him going for long hours. Laurie and I live nine hundred miles away.

Although we don't like the current arrangement none of us wants to put Dad in a rest home. He was in one right after the stroke and it was a horrible, awful place. He was so unhappy he seemed to be willing himself to die. He wouldn't eat. I don't blame him. They would take him into the dining room with no clothes on, just wrapped in a sheet. There was no dignity left.

So the folks are in that apartment with no friends around, except Art and Jill. Laurie and I try to visit regularly, coming for five days in alternate months. While we are there Mom is fine. She still gets depressed, but stays pretty positive until we leave. Then she cries. This is our main problem, trying to keep Mom happy. She feels like this is the end of the road for her. Dad could live for years and by then she'll be too old to even enjoy life. Mom also worries about what would happen if Dad should out- live her.

Being a caretaker is not only hard because it is a twenty-four hour job, but it's hard because your whole way of life has to change.

I believe everyone is doing their share. David drives over two mornings a week to shave Dad, give him a shower and trim his hair . He takes good care of Dad. Laurie still has young children at home and her job at the library, but she reschedules her life to come and stay. Even though I don't work and my children are gone I have to do some juggling, arrange for people to water the lawn, teach my Sunday School class, things like that.

I do wonder if Jill and Art visit often enough. Mom complains that somedays Jill doesn't even come at all. Yet, I realize they have the brunt of the problem at their doorstep all the time. I can't really fault anyone.

But we all feel we should have been consulted about moving the folks. We might have been able to keep them in their old home and hire adequate help. We should have at least talked it over first.

Three of us, Laurie, David and I, find it very easy to talk together. Jill is different. She seems to live with a different reality. If we make suggestions she ignores us. Since she was "that high" Jill has been a loner. Now she seems to shun us. She always has some project, something on her mind, claiming her attention.

We three are always trying to figure out how to best approach Jill. We'd like to know if her new job is going to continue to require long hours. Art's job has taken him out of the state. This spring he was away for three different weeks. Mom gets nervous and scared, especially at night. What if something would happen? What if Dad needed help or what if there were a fire? Who would she call? What would she do?

If we moved Mom and Dad out of the apartment we'd probably never be able to speak to Jill and Art again, they'd be so angry. We have to work around this situation and make the best of it.

Last Labor Day weekend we were all together so I organized a work party. The apartment needs some fixing. There are unpacked boxes all over the place. They don't know what to do with all their antiques. They don't have their pictures hung up on the walls. The kitchen isn't organized. There were plenty of adults and teenagers ready to help. But Art got tied up with his business. Jill seemed distracted and unable to cooperate. I kept asking for suggestions and help. Finally she said, "I don't like people arranging things, putting things away, when they are not going to be here to work with the folks." That made me angry. It seemed a good time to get things done.

So I just took over and directed the kids to put things here, hang a picture there. Jill left and we didn't see her the rest of the afternoon. Later Mom told me that Art and Jill felt I was taking over, bossing everyone. I can't believe how angry that made me feel. Jill could have been the foreman.

The tensions over this situation continue. We don't agree, but we don't have many choices. We try to choose the "least worst" alternative, and then afterwards get another idea and wonder why we didn't think of that sooner. I don't know if any other choice would have been better. Looking back on it, maybe another way would have been just as bad.

**Jill and Art**

Jill: When we moved the folks, everybody had their opinions, but they weren't here. Laurie now says, "I wish you had consulted us before moving them. We would have told you not to do it." They forget that Dad has serious medical needs. He must visit the physical therapist regularly. He and Mom need help daily, just to get Dad in and out of bed.

David was too undependable. It was too far for me to drive daily out to where they lived.

Art: Mom balked at it, but we carried through with the move. It seemed the most important thing at the time; Dad's health and welfare were at stake. He needed to be in a place where he'd get good treatment.

Jill: Now Mom calls David and Ellen, and they call Barb, and Barb calls Laurie, all because Mom is unhappy. I've never met anyone who worries as much as my mother. If there isn't something to fuss over in the immediate family, she worries about the neighbors, or starving children in other countries.

Mother loved being in the suburbs. And she lived in the limelight of the floral shop for years, hearing nothing but praise at how wonderful David was, how great her artistic arrangements were. She lived on this; it was her life, her breath. And when that ended she couldn't handle it.

I go down to their house in the morning and say, "Hi Dad. I'm going to bring you some good breakfast this morning. Come on, sit up. I'm going to wash your face." I do everything to be positive. Mother gets negative and argues with Dad. And when Barb and Laurie come Mom complains saying, "What will I do if Dad gets worse? What if something breaks?

I'm stuck here in this apartment, and I'm lonely, and everything is terrible."

If only Mother could stop worrying. She makes absolutely no effort to change her attitude, to make life pleasant.

Art: Dad has not been a problem. He has been a model patient, easy to manipulate. Mom has been the perennial trial.

Jill: Yes. I feel I am trying to appease some horrible combination dictator and martyr who gets angry one minute and sulks the next.

Holidays don't turn out to be pleasant family gatherings. They turn into a three day fiasco. Everyone comes from all directions and for days you are feeding all these people. Everyone is running everywhere, tempers are short, and emotions are high.

Barb comes and tells me how unhappy Mother is. Then she'll say, "Now we are going to get this organized. I'm going to have one of my boys carry up the boxes from the storage room so we can sort things out."

Yesterday Barb had ten of us working to organize the apartment. She started acting like a drill sergeant. "Why isn't this done?" "You can't let Mother do that." "Why is Dad in bed so early?"

I can't take these jabs all the time. I can't handle it anymore. I'm too emotional. I've got things on my mind. I can't understand Barb's temper.

Laurie has said, "It's just not working out for Mother. She's so unhappy. If you'd just stop once in a while and visit with her."

Does she think I drive past there and I don't stop? Until I went back to work three months ago, I was there day and night. I spent at least five hours every day with the folks. I'd help Mother get breakfast because it took her forever, she moves so slow. She is getting to the point where she forgets she has something on the stove and walks away. The food burns, but she feeds it to Dad anyway. He gets mad and yells at her, telling her it is garbage. So they argue.

For two months after the folks moved here, David, who lives just seventeen miles away, never drove over to see them. Mother would make excuses, saying, "They have a business." So, we don't have a business? We don't have to work? Mother has always been protective of "little David." He's so wonderful. And, "poor Laurie and Barb. They live so far away."

They may live far away, but when they come they feel free to be critical.

Art: I have a new business in real estate. If people call and can't get hold of me, they take their business to another agent. I gave three months to helping the folks. I found the apartment, arranged for the move, sat with Dad, took him to a specialist. But I couldn't keep doing this. I got five months behind in my house payments and everything seemed to be going under. I had to go to work. But I found I couldn't be away from here for more than three hours at a time without Mom saying, "Oh, where were you? I didn't know what to do."

Jill has had health problems and can't do much lifting. When I'm gone she can't lift Dad by herself. The family has finally started to kick in some money to pay for a nurse to come every morning and evening to help.

Jill: When Laurie and Barb come they both come at once so they can have a vacation together. That doesn't help me.

Art: I felt like a traitor when I went out of the state for job training, but it was essential.

Jill: When Barb comes she brings Mother lovely gifts. My brother and sisters have money. I can't complete with them. Mother raves about how wonderful Barbara is, how talented Laurie and David are. I feel so hurt.

All these negative feelings have just surfaced. They came when Mother started comparing children. I still have "mommy" dreams at age fifty-five. No matter what I do I can't seem to win my mother's approval. When I vent my feelings Mother says I am going to cause her and Dad to have strokes and heart attacks and die. So now that guilt will be on my head if it happens.

Last night we had a big family fight and I feel like I've lost everything. Afterwards I told Art I'd like to kill myself. I've lost my brother. I've lost my sisters. I've lost my folks. My kids are driving me nuts. I have nobody left. I hate my boss, I hate my job. What do I have? I feel terrible.

Chapter 11

# The Spirit Trail

Evelyn Corn, an educated woman with an Ed.D, grew up on an Indian reservation in the Midwest. The family had lived in a one room log cabin with no plumbing, no electricity, none of the conveniences. Her mother had encouraged each of the five children to grow beyond these humble conditions. Evelyn, who spent a summer helping her mother die, hoped that in her final days her mother recognized and felt some comfort in what she had accomplished.

My sister Sadie called in April and said, "I think you better come over and spend some time with Mom. It doesn't look good. We don't know when she'll take the spirit trail."

Mother had been born into a wealthy, religious family on the East coast. She was a twin, whose mother hemorrhaged and died giving birth. Her father blamed her, as the second to be delivered, for this death. He could not accept her. He continued his rejection of her his whole life, especially after she married an Indian. As a result she never felt the love of either parent.

This made me marvel all the more at what a good mother she was. Although she never had a role model, she somehow captured the essence of motherhood. She enjoyed being a mother; she wanted her children. She took great joy in seeing us unfold and grow, in teaching us to be independent thinkers.

Mother knew that being of Indian descent might limit our opportunities. Being of mixed blood, too, we would not really be accepted by either side. So she found opportunities for us to offset the deficiencies of living on a reservation.

I asked her once, "How did you get to be such a good mother?" She said, "I always wanted to be the mother I never had."

Trained as a Public Health nurse, Mother worked as a field nurse on the Rosebud reservation; the only health professional at Parmalee, South Dakota, in the early 1930's.

Mother was not an Indian; she was of English descent. But her heart was all Indian. She joked about having a quart of Indian in her. She had needed a transfusion after the birth of one of her children. My father's blood type had matched hers so he donated the blood she needed.

Mother loved the Indian people and worked for them all her life. About twenty years ago a major change in reservation life was instigated. No one had consulted the common Indian about it. Mother saw the change as politically motivated and vowed to do something about it. She started writing letters. At night, in our small log cabin, she would type letters to senators in Washington, to state people, to Indian organizations across the country. On the weekend, when the rest of the family might be at the border town to shop or to see a movie, she would be at home, working by kerosene lamp, typing letters.

Something unusual happened to Mother during this time. We lived right beside a river. One night while she was at the typewriter she saw lights moving toward the cabin. They came from a corner of the field where there used to be a grave site. These lights came in through the window, passed across her hands, and shot off down the bank toward the river. The lights left her with a warm, glowing feeling. She named them Spirit Lights.

On another occasion the Spirit Lights came again. She was driving her old jalopy on a dirt road that led to the homes of some women friends. Although these friends had passed on to the Spirit Trail, they were women Mother felt close to, women who had talked with her about the Indian reservation problems.

It was a foggy evening, so foggy she couldn't see. The Spirit Lights appeared in front of the car, moving back and forth, seeming to guide her. She felt they were reaffirming that she was right. They were telling her to continue going down that trail, to continue using her skills in working for Indians.

I thought of these things as I drove the five hundred miles to visit Mother following Sadie's phone call.

When I arrived Mother wanted to go for a ride around the reservation. We drove north along the river. We walked slowly in the woods, listened to the river rapids, heard the chipmunks scurrying, the crows cawing. It was her last taste of freedom in the outdoors, a most treasured experience. She had had to move to the city to live with her daughter and could no longer roam the woods. Cancer forced her indoors, taking her mobility and her independence.

I soon had to go back to my job, but came out again the first of June. Mother asked to go back out to South Dakota again to hear the drums. This wasn't possible. She couldn't really travel anymore. She was too weak and she needed to be near a bathroom.

I didn't even have a tape of Powwow music to play for her. I don't know why I never thought to ask someone for one.

My sister Mary and I did drive Mother to the reservation to visit a special friend, a Reverend who had helped her. He had brought her back to the church. After being rejected by her conservative, religious father, Mother had cut off all ties with her family. Deciding white man's religion didn't do any good, she determined to follow the Indian way. But people don't lose their early values. Eventually she integrated and lived both Indian and Christian values. Her philosophy served as a model for her children, encouraging us to adjust to both cultures.

My son and daughter had come with me for the summer. Marvin, who had just returned from a year in Yugoslavia as an exchange student, was especially good with his Grandmother. He loved reading the Bible and talking with Mother about religious concepts. He would say, "We want you to stay with us as long as you can, but remember the Father has many rooms in his house and is preparing one for you, at this very minute." Hoping to reinforce this positive view I would add, "Mom, you've never seen your mother before. We are all wondering what she looks like. When you go over there to see her you must remember that when it is our time we will follow you and see both of you." We were trying to make her transition, her dying, easier for her.

Mother knew she was losing life. She was coming to the time when she could no longer talk. Her lungs were filling up with fluid, and it was difficult to breathe. The doctor told us she would get pneumonia in the end and stop breathing. We tried to use her own words so she would feel most comforted. We found ourselves saying "Spirit Lights", "Spirit Trail", "We'll meet you when it is our turn," over and over again.

But there was too much of an unknown on the other side. Mother wanted to stay here. Her fear was evident. She was turning more and more childlike. It wasn't because she didn't have courage. She had courage her whole life.

Her cancer was eating at her body and her pancreatic area was a great big, swollen ball. It was such a devastating condition. Other people get emaciated from the disease, but she grew larger.

Knowing that Mother needed reassurance, we always touched her. We held on to her hand. And I gave her baths. She loved having a bath. I lifted her into the tub by myself, as long as I could. When I could no longer lift her--I almost dropped her once--I told her it was time for us to have some help.

My sisters and I talked to Mother about going to a nursing home. Sadie worked as a nurse and Mary lectured at the local university. We couldn't all be home at the same time and couldn't really take care of her. She fought it all the way. We finally had to do it in spite of her protests. As we put her in the car Sadie told her, "Mom, we are taking you to the nursing home." Mother moaned and cried, "No." We assured her we'd be right with her, but she was beyond reason. It was such a pitiful moment. Tears were streaming down our faces. It was wrenching.

Mother was in the home about two weeks. I stayed there with her for hours at a time. I always touched her and I always rubbed her feet as I talked to her. Even if she couldn't talk she could feel the sensation.

One time, toward the end, all five of us were gathered around her bed. (I hoped Mother could realize that her dream for her children had been fulfilled. All of us had received an education and were working for Indian rights.) But Mary spoiled the moment by saying something about what we would do when Mother died. I told her to be quiet. Mary answered, "Mother can't hear us." "Shut up," I said, "she can too." I looked over at Mother's face. Two large tears spilled out of her eyes. I am sure she had heard.

Summer was over. Mother's death was imminent, but she was still hanging on. I hated to leave, but I had to take my children back home to school. I wanted to bathe my Mother one more time. The nurses at the home said they would do it. One volunteered to give her a sponge bath. But I wanted to do it myself. I carried her down the hallway to the tub. I gently washed her body, supporting her head so she could relax in the water. I dried her and put powder on her skin. She always liked that. It was a tender moment. I felt I was preparing her for her funeral.

I asked Sadie not to let Mother know I was leaving. It would only cause her anxiety. Sadie didn't agree with me. She said, "I've always been honest and open with Mother." If I had known Sadie was going to tell Mom, I would have spent time assuring Mother that I would be back. I didn't even want her to know I was going. I believe Mother gave up--feeling that one of us, seemingly, was giving up on her.

This was mid-August and I had been there, day after day, since early June. I didn't realize it at the time--I was so stressed from the caretaking--but I was quite ill. A bronchial infection was draining my energy; I was extremely weak. Still, we had to leave. We really couldn't wait any longer.

We got a late start. Marvin drove. I was in the back seat of the car trying to relax and thinking of Mother lying in her bed.

We had been riding for a while when I glanced at the car clock. It was 7:30 p.m. Putting my head back, I closed my eyes, and silently said these simple words, "Father, take your daughter in her sleep without pain." As I said this I saw my mother's face and felt her presence. I didn't think anything of this because she was constantly on my mind.

The next morning when I phoned my sisters to see how Mother was, Mary could hardly speak. I knew something had happened. Sadie came to the phone and said, "Mom passed on about 7:30 last night."

I thought, "Oh, that's what that was. My mother had come to see me." At the moment that she was meeting her own mother, the Great Spirit had joined us all together.

Mother's body was cremated and her ashes spread in the woods near the river, a place she loved.

Chapter 12

# Mom, Then Dad

Nancy Jackson is a professional woman who holds an administrative position at a large university in the West. When her parents suffered strokes, she wanted to provide them with the best medical care and therapy possible. She is doing for her father what she was unable to do for her mother.

## Mother's Story

I was the light of my mother's life. I think all of her children felt the same way. Mother could do that--make you feel special for no other reason except that you were you. My father was different. He expected his children to learn, to do, to be productive. Mother, on the other hand, offered unconditional love.

When Mother died four years ago I did so much grieving, not because she died, but because I didn't feel I had done what I could to make her last years comfortable. I still weep when I think about it.

My mother was an absolute jewel. She bore nine children, owned and operated a small town grocery store, and in addition, catered to Dad's every whim. She was loving and giving to everyone, but especially to Dad. He expected this. Dad, as the thirteenth child, had received considerable attention while growing up. From what I've heard he was the apple of everyone's eye. Everyone loved him. He was energetic; he got up singing every morning. He had a strong, outgoing personality, and he expected much from those around him. Mother, on the other hand, was the kind of person who loved you for what you were. It was Mother's love, strength, and compassion that held the family together.

Five years ago Mother had a mastectomy followed by a stroke, or a series of strokes. In her frailty I felt extremely protective of her. Living in a small town in Idaho, she couldn't get the kind of care she needed. I insisted she come to Salt Lake City to see specialists for rehabilitative care. The doctor there was wonderful, talking to Mother after her mastectomy, and helping her through the whole thing, helping her feel good about herself.

Then something happened; she lost her ability to speak. It seems most cruel to me to see people treat those with a physical disability as though they have a mental problem. People around Mother would say, "She's losing her mind." This was traumatic for Mother and heartbreaking for me; having people act as though, since she couldn't answer them, she must be losing her mental capacities. Her local doctor seemed to believe there was nothing to be done; it was a problem with the brain.

Dad accepted the doctor's analysis, feeling that it was just a matter of time till Mother died. I couldn't accept this. Again, I had Mother come and stay with me so she could go for speech therapy. She was here three or four weeks, but she wasn't happy away from Dad. Mother needed to be by Dad. She wanted to be there for him, so she returned to Idaho.

Because of the nature of my parent's relationship, I knew Mother wasn't going to get much attention or support from Dad. I tried to give that positive help from a distance. I phoned two or three times a week. I would say, "What are you telling yourself when you get up in the morning? Mother, I want you to go to the mirror right now and say 'good morning' to yourself." I'd give her short phrases to repeat, to keep the speech therapy going.

Then a series of minor strokes further diminished her abilities, her dignity. Both a lack of positive encouragement and side effects from medication contributed to unnecessary problems. Mother had diarrhea, and no one seemed to feel anything could be done. She, herself, seemed resigned to ill health. This didn't seem right to me. I called one doctor and then another, explaining the symptoms and listing the medications. Finally a doctor told me the diarrhea was a side effect of medication and wondered why she was still using one particular drug. A new prescription cured the problem.

Older people need an advocate. They, and often those around them, tend to accept what is happening. They accept what the doctor says without questioning and without searching for better solutions.

A great conflict for me was whether I should give up my job to go care for my mother or make some other arrangements. In the summer I could move home and devote my time to Mother, day and night. But I didn't start soon enough. I believe Mother would be alive today if she had come to live with me. I wish I had made my parents move here. They could have been together, and Mother would have had the care she deserved.

During the last two years of Mother's life I drove to Idaho every other weekend, a six-hour drive. I would leave Friday at noon and return Sunday evening. I wanted to comfort her, to tend to her needs, to keep her life interesting and full of love. I'd make my Mother laugh by dancing around the room for her. I am not a dancer, but I'd whirl and twirl and pose and say, "Aren't I wonderful? With my natural talent, think what I'd have been if I'd had lessons." We'd both laugh.

I did everything to keep her alive. When she had lost all her capabilities, I was still pushing food down. Even when she got to where her throat was paralyzed, I could find food that would roll down. She would do anything to please me. Finally the family said, "Nancy, you have to let Mother die." I knew this had to happen, but it grieved me greatly. I was not sure that everything possible that could have been done had been done--even things that might have been against her will.

Mother died the 4th of September. I always work through the lunch hour, but on that day I told the secretary I was going to take a break. My thoughts were on Mother and I needed to get away from the office. I went home and while standing at the kitchen sink, looking out the window, I experienced a very strong connection with Mother. I found myself saying out loud, "Mother, you've just got to let go. You've got to go. Everything will be all right." I wept over these words even as I said them, but I knew somehow I needed to say them. About fifteen minutes later the phone rang with the news that Mother had just passed away. It seemed I had to let her go. My strength had sustained her this last summer of her life and it was my strength that had to let her go. I had not been able to let her die while I was with her.

My personal struggle was in trying to understand why my mother, who had been so good and compassionate, so gracious and giving all her life, had had to suffer in her dying.

I am still touched, moved to tears, by this memory. Mother struggled all her life through physical and financial hardships. There were never any frills. It seemed immensely sad to me that this struggle never ended. Seeing her pain was heart-breaking. It was reflected in her face as she suffered small strokes. But when I'd ask, "Mother, do you hurt?" she would smile and say no.

I learned much from her death. I witnessed the overwhelming will of the mortal body to live, to not give up. One has no idea of what the physical body can endure. When I saw my mother dwindle to fifty-six pounds. . .

Her illness left her weak, robbed of dignity. Still, there was dignity in the struggle. Mother was so beautiful those last few months, her white hair framing her face. One by one, her children came home, to visit, to say goodbye. It seemed she lived long enough to allow each of her children to discover a deeper meaning in life by seeing the suffering of her mortal body, and then to see the beauty of death in her release from suffering.

**Dad's story:**

Dad's stroke came while Mother was still alive. His right side was paralyzed, but this didn't affect his speech or his mind, just his body. My goal became to ensure a quality life style for Dad. I determined to do for Dad what I hadn't done soon enough for Mother.

I knew I would have to get help, and this wasn't possible in his small, farm community. There was no one willing to take the responsibility of being the caretaker. Everyone was afraid something serious might happen. Besides, there wasn't any physical therapy available. So I brought Dad to live with me.

I share a house with three other professional women. These women are wonderful with Dad. One of them is willing to share her bedroom with me so Dad can have my room. I don't ask these women to participate in caring for Dad, but they happily spend time with him as though he were their own Dad. All of us are busy with our jobs, but if I have something special coming up and ask ahead, they are generous with their time. They have the same family values I have and don't resent my wanting to help my father.

I give Dad my Saturdays and Sundays and my weekday evenings. I plan activities for him on a daily basis. Instead of having him just watch the football game on television, and he does plenty of that, I arrange to get him in a wheelchair and out to all home games. He goes to all the women's tennis and volleyball home games also.

I learned from Mother's situation and am trying to implement this knowledge as I care for my father. I learned how much pre-planning is necessary. Caretakers must have relief--respite, a break, recreational activities, some association with friends outside this situation--or they won't be able to continue. And every caretaker needs a list of people to call on. That list can never be too long and it has to be constantly updated. Too often the person becomes overwhelmed by the problem and determines he cannot do the job. What caretakers need is sufficient planning to give them time away so they won't end up feeling, "Poor me."

I have two women who alternate coming in during the daytime. I use many university students. They have the enthusiasm and professional attitude that makes life interesting for Dad. I even call on the neighbor boy to come play a game of Rummy Cube with Dad during the evening if I have other things to do.

I decided early on that it wasn't worth it to make a fuss over accidents, like spilling the urinal, dropping food, etc. Why be critical of those whose physical abilities are not as sharp anymore? I put down a rug with a good backing that can be easily picked up and washed. I provide a supply of napkins and aprons for meal times. Dad is very particular about his appearance. He wears stylish clothing, shaves daily and uses men's cologne so he smells good.

Dad is mentally alert. He loves his church work, and I have made certain he can, with some assistance, continue in it. Still, I fight the negative attitudes people hold toward the handicapped. Once, when I couldn't get away, I had a friend take him to the Temple. They were turned away; told it wasn't possible for someone in a wheelchair. Instead of accepting that, I called back and checked to see what the policy was. The President assured me Dad was welcome and that, indeed, there were people who could give him the help he needed.

Dad has been able to change a little these past years. He wasn't sympathetic or sufficiently helpful when Mother became ill. He's more understanding now that he, too, has suffered a stroke. Dad can be critical of people who don't do things the way he thinks they should be done, or don't live up to his standards. He was upset with me once over something I had done, or not done, and I said, "Dad, there are a hundred ways to do things and this isn't worth fussing about. If we are going to get along you can't fret over little, unimportant matters." I've heard Dad repeat this sentiment to others since then. I feel at ease with my father, now. He has become more accepting.

A great thing about Dad is that he gives back to the people around him. He has a positive attitude and shares it with others, encouraging people--those who have been hired as aides--to realize their dreams, to dare to do things they really want to do. Dad feels he has a mission, and his mission is to help others. Wherever we go, he initiates conversations and seeks to know and encourage people.

I want Dad to be in control of his own life. He continues to work at his own physical therapy. He takes his non-working arm and moves it with the strong arm. The same with his legs. Even with this diligent fitness regime there is a continual loss of muscle tone.

I realize I am Dad's sense of security and try to relieve unnecessary tension and worry. When his medication causes internal bleeding or when he loses his ability to walk, we work together to find solutions. I know there will come a time when I will have to provide professional health care for Dad. He will be too heavy for me to lift. I believe he will take his cheerful disposition into that new situation. Meanwhile I am happy organizing for Dad's care. Things are working out fine.

Afterword

## The Caretakers

### Support for the caretaker

The caregivers whose stories are reported here are emotionally stable individuals able and willing to provide support and care. Strong feelings of love and concern are communicated. There are no revelations of elder abuse. Few even admit to themselves the extent of their frustration at the endlessness of the task and the embarrassment of inappropriate behavior from their parents. What is evident is the common thread of concern for the parent and anxiety over making good decisions. The stories "Shared Caring" and "Not A Relative" are remarkable accounts of caregivers going beyond what anyone might reasonably expect.

However, none of the caretaking was free of tension. The emotional strings that connect parent and child are invisible, but in most cases they are strong and long-lasting. One middle-aged woman, who brought her father into her home because he was dying of cancer, was amazed to feel a resurfacing of emotions she had experienced as a child. She was in constant fear that she might trigger her father's anger, the intense, irrational anger she recalled from her childhood.

Another caretaker, a counselor by profession, was surprised to discover how unrealistic his expectations were regarding his mother. He could not accept her senility. Her constant requests for things that were impossible, her repetitive, illogical conversations, made him furious.

When the caregiver feels what seem to be childish emotions coming into play he feels confused and angry. Struggling with these emotions is just one more facet of the caretaking situations that makes the caretaker feel guilty. There are additional factors.

The term "the sandwich generation" refers to those caught in the middle (see "Mother's Last Days"). With women waiting longer to have children it is possible to have a forty-year-old working mother, breast feeding her first child, and also being responsible for an ill or aging parent. And, with increased longevity, it is also possible that a sixty-two year old grandmother may be the one in the middle.

One such woman complained, "I don't know what to do. I had to leave early this morning to tend the grandchildren and my mother didn't get dressed until 4:00 p.m. If I'm not there to encourage her she doesn't do much but sleep. I can't help my daughter with her children, fix meals for my husband and also keep Mother active. There isn't enough of me to do all that."

Often the primary caretaker works full-time outside the home and takes on the responsibility as an added load. Many of those interviewed were in this position. These caretakers, most of them women, need recognition and support. While they may value the chance to talk to others and share ideas and support, many find themselves too busy to want to attend another meeting.

Caretakers everywhere need encouragement and guidance. And they need help in recognizing the costs--physical, financial and emotional--in assuming the caretaker role. Written material, media attention, and a greater community awareness may give them some of the support they need. Any information that guides in making intelligent choices will relieve some of the confusion and stress that accompanies the caregiving responsibilities.

Information related to caring for the elderly is available in an increasing number of books and magazine articles. A short annotated bibliography following this chapter cites a few of them.

The range of topics covered in these books is broad and the focus of each is slightly different, but they all have valuable information, and in addition each contains extensive references.

**Learn as You Go**

Because no two cases are alike, and because there is continual change within each situation, there can be no formula for successfully planning the care of aging adults. Circumstances change, sometimes slowly, sometimes suddenly and drastically. Caretakers must learn as they go, make changes when necessary, and avoid blaming themselves when they don't anticipate every problem in advance.

Those responsible for aging adults must recognize that their parents may need ever-increasing assistance. As the situation changes they will have to face their own limitations--those of time as well as emotional and financial resources. They must remind themselves frequently that they are doing the best they can, that there are no miracle answers and that, in fact, they are performing a generous and loving act.

Appendix

## Annotated Bibliography

This bibliography is not intended to be all inclusive. Most of the books listed have excellent references to lead the reader to additional material that includes a listing of agencies, places to write, suggestions about where to turn for help.

**Books:**

Greenberg, Vivian E. *Your Best is Good Enough.* Lexington, Mass.: Lexington Books, 125 Spring Street, 1989. $16.95.

The author, a social worker, is promoting better communication between the caregiver and the adult receiving the care. She writes about things people often feel uncomfortable saying. Speaking for the parents, she suggests they want to be part of any decision made about their lives, like changes in diet, living quarters, health care. And they want to hang on to the symbols of their independence, such as the car or the bank account, even when they can no longer use them. The author also speaks for the caregivers suggesting they do what they can, hire help to do the things they can't manage, assess the situation to determine if they are doing what really needs doing, and then to stop feeling guilty about things they can't change.

Halphern, James, Ph.D. *Helping Your Aging Parents; a Practical Guide for Adult Children.* N.Y.: Fawcett Crest, 1987. 335 pp.

An excellent source of information, this book combines facts and figures with case histories that illustrate the stress and emotional factors in caregiving. There is a chapter explaining family systems theory, one on nursing homes, another on death and funerals, and a listing of state and local agencies on aging. The print is small, but headings are clear and the price is right ($4.95).

Jacobsen, Jamia Jasper, Editor. *Help! I'm Parenting My Parents*. Benchmark Press, Inc., 1988. 325 pp.

Contains material by twenty different authors whose backgrounds range from lawyer to social worker to pharmacist. Included are chapters on nutrition, pets, financial planning, elder abuse, wellness and exercise, and crime prevention. There is also a chapter that explains home health care services and one that discusses making the nursing home decision. This book contains some materials not found in other texts. The language is non-technical.

MacLean, Helene. *Caring for Your Parents: A Sourcebook of Options and Solutions for Both Generations*. Garden City, NY: Doubleday & Company, Inc., 1987. 370 pp.

Comprehensive and readable. Includes sections on family conferences, finances, living wills, health and safety ideas. Also offers suggestions for dealing with loneliness and boredom. There is information on travel, the Elderhostel program, drugs, the pharmacist, health insurance, quackery, adult day care, home care, nursing homes and a state-by-state listing of agencies and resources.

Otten, Jane and Florence D. Shelley, *When Your Parents Grow Old*. Revised and updated. NY: Signet, 1978. Also in hard cover by Funk and Wagnalls. 291 pp.

Another excellent resource covering a broad range of possible problems and possible solutions. There are ideas for helping parents when you are far away as well as suggestions on counseling for their marital problems. Chapter topics range from money matters, to doctors, diseases, the healthy aged, and where to find help. Sections within chapters touch on such practical considerations as how to visit aging parents, how to avoid crisis situations, morale, safety, stages of dependencies, etc. Appendices list helping agencies and where to write.

Poe, William D., M.D. *The Old Person in Your Home*. Charles Scribner's Sons, 1969. 180 pp.

Although published before the development of cardiopulmonary resuscitation (CPR) and the increase in services for the elderly, the direct, non-technical language of the book, and the short to-the-point chapters addressing pertinent questions make this book worthwhile. Forty-six chapters cover topics from understanding the elderly to death and the funeral arrangements.

Schwartz, Dr. Arthur N. *Survival Handbook for Children of Aging Parents.* Chicago: Follett Publishing Co., 1977. 160 pp.

Conversational in style, this book contains non-technical, broadly applicable information and guide- lines. Discusses the ideas that old age can be a productive and enriching period, that senility may be a mask, and that transitions are always stressful. Also discusses institutionalization and death and dying.

**Magazine Articles:**

There are a growing number of magazine articles written on the subject of caretaking for the aging. Included here are only a few. The first one stresses the emotional aspect, the other three, all part of a special report, give more facts.

Civia Tamarkin, "A Home Not Her Own," *People Weekly,* Oct. 3, 1988, pp. 100-111.

A touching story of the stress felt by both the mother and the son when it became necessary to move the mother into a nursing home. The ending suggests that after several tension-filled weeks, the mother is beginning to adjust to her new situation. Photographs tell much of the story.

Augustin Hedberg," Caring for Your Aging Parents," *Money,* Oct. 1989, pp. 138-145.

Lani Luciano, "Finding Health Care and Housing," *Money,* Oct. 1989, pp. 158-166.

Margaret T. Smith, "The Best Ways to Help Financially", *Money,* Oct. 1989, pp. 148-152.

**AARP**

One additional resource of particular value to the long distance caregiver is provided by the Social Outreach and Support Program Departmentof the American Association of Retired Persons.

Write for a free copy:

"Miles Away and Still Caring" D12748
AARP Fulfillment
1909 K Street, N.W.
Washington, DC, 20049

This handbook contains three sections:

Identifying the Informal Support System--friends or relatives who already are providing some help.

Expanding the Roles of Existing Support Systems--asking those already involved to take on additional tasks, and identifying others who are willing to be involved.

Locating and using Formal Services--finding professional help in your relative's community.

## Order Form

Call 1-800-456-7770
or write:
UniPress
2020 Kansas Drive
Brookings, South Dakota, 57006
Phone (605) 692-9750

Please send the following:

| | |
|---|---|
| **We've Got To Do Something About Mother** | $8.95 |
| Shipping and handling | $1.25 |
| S.D. residents add %5 sales tax | .45 |

No. of copies ______ Total enclosed ________

Also available:

| | |
|---|---|
| **Women, Houses and Homes:** an anthology of prose, poetry, photography. Eleven women from the Midwest share their memories and/or philosophies about home. | $6.00 |
| Shipping and handling | 1.25 |
| S.D. residents add %5 sales tax | .30 |

No. of copies______ Total enclosed_________